by: Nolan "Dino" Hall

Transcribed by: Tina Perry

Edited by: April Smiley

DO UNTO OTHERS

MP

MOCY PUBLISHING
WWW.MOCYPUBLISHING.COM

Detroit, Michigan

Do Unto Others

ISBN 978-1-940831-03-9
Copyright © 2013 by Nolan "Dino" Hall

Published by Mocy Publishing, LLC.
Website: www.mocypublishing.com
Email: info@mocypublishing.com
Phone: (313) 436-6944

FOREWORD

Stone and Allen are young men, yet they've come up through the streets owning several businesses. Things come crashing down around them when Allen's brother Spook gets out of Jackson State prison and brings death to their inner circle.

A greedy and sinister drug King pin, Herbert T. Stone comes to town. Hate and Vengeance on his mind, believing Spook to be responsible for the death of his sister. As the knot gets tighter Stone and Allen find out that Herbert T. had plans for them even before Spook was released from prison. Stone's soon to be wife tomorrow is kidnapped. Spooked is desperately being looked for by his brother and people who want him dead as he goes on his stick-up spree, with two females. Who will ride or die for him. Drug induced thoughts and sexual bliss is all the two women want out of life.

After Stone's loved ones start coming up missing a man of Spook's caliber is seriously needed to deal with the deadly threat. They all soon learn that you can't separate the ones you love from the choices you make.

AUTHOR'S NOTE

Although this book "Do Unto Others", is based on some true accounts, I would like to acknowledge that the incidents and depiction of characters and places are not founded on personal or firsthand accounts, but more so on a compilation of verified occurrences collected from non-related sources. This book is also is embellished with an added story line to present a full work.

I would like to thank all of the people who took the time to read this story. Some may even view is as hard hitting or a bit abrasive, unfortunately its some peoples way of life. It is my humble opinion that adversity in some form or degree stunts or promotes growth in our lives, it's how we come through the other side of adversity that makes us weak or stronger.

Kindest Regards,

Nolan "Dino" Hall

ACKNOWLEDGEMENTS

I give praise and Thanks to the author and finisher of all, God the almighty and most high. May his mercy and grace endure forever.

I give much love, thanks and honor to my wonderful parents, Noise and Pearl Hall, for nurturing me with much love and care. For being there for me when the world wasn't so kind. My only sister Carolyn Taylor, I love you! May God bless and rest your souls. I wish you well in the hereafter and send my heartfelt love.

Much love and embraces to my multitude of loved ones, who help me to flourish. My Children, Dawanna, Takishanne, Erica, Nolan, Victor, Swann, Jacquelyn and Mario, daddy loves you with all of his heart.

Exceptionally intense feeling and appreciation to Dawayne, Chavez, and Vicki Hall. Also to Chrystal Thomas, Felay Smith, Maria Murphy, Michelle Henke, Johnny Collins, Janel McElmurry, Gloria Beechum, Terence Brooks, Ronnie Hawkins, Roy Traylor, and Hope Anderson for encouraging words and not giving up on me. To all of you I bestow my profound love and devotion.

Special thanks to Demetrius L. Favors, Tommy and Barbara Bradley, You've been a blessing and you have my gratitude and kindest regards.

Much Thanks and big ups to Lamont William and Donele "Casino" Bailey, I wish you both continued success.

Susan Meiburg, I give thanks for assisting me in fighting my legal battle and Ronald Wilson Sr. for his contributions in typing. Also thank you Henry Charles Davis (Commonly Known as "Chuck"), John "Kid" Hall and D. Stewart-EL (.A.K.A Big Dame), Marlon "Smooth" Holland and Eric Oneil Woods for being there.

CHARACTERS

Stone – An ex addict who has had his share of hardships, reaches his bottom with drugs, cleans up his life, and builds a small empire.

Allen – Stone's business partner, his best and trusted friend. They help each other stay on their feet.

Tomorrow – Stone's beautiful woman who owns a lucrative beauty shop.

Carol- Allen's lovely woman, Tomorrow's best friend, and co- owner of the beauty shop.

Delsena- A chocolate beauty, she's rich, has a smart head on her shoulders , and owns a chain of restaurants that was willed to her by her dead parents. She loves Stone and wants Stone to wed her, but Tomorrow stands in her way.

Spook- Allen's brother, fresh out of prison. He wants money, fast and will take it.
He upsets the harmonious balance of Stone and Allen's plush lifestyle, bringing problems and trouble, being the thuggish gangsta that he is.

Herbert T. – A ruthless drug dealer from Stone's past. He seeks revenge when all things point to Spook for the death of his family member.

PROLOGUE

He saw the fist coming at his face. His brain signaled his body to move. Too late. Stone was knocked from the bar stool to the floor. He tasted the metallic flavor of the blood from his busted lip. The bar he was thick with smoke from cigarettes, cigars, and poor ventilation. Plus the music was uncomfortably loud. Stone tried getting to his feet, only to be kicked in the side by the second guy. The two men grabbed and dragged him outside to the back of the alley. Onlookers watched in fear, not wanting anything to do with these ruthless thugs that worked for dope dealers. Once they had him outside, the two henchmen went back to work on him.

Stone tried to recover and throw a few punches oh his own, but too many days and nights of drinking and drugging had dulled his senses and zapped his strength. His strength seemed to be non- existent. His body absorbed much of the punishment each blow brought immense pain upon impact. Stone was now in survival mode. It was because of his drug use that brought about the unfortunate beating he now received. Stone owed and couldn't pay. Now the payment was being taken out on his ass. What seemed like forever to him was finally over, as he laid there barely conscious among the garbage, papers, and broken glass that littered this urine stenched alley. Blood was hemorrhaging from his mouth and ear.

Stone watched the two men leave through his swollen eyes while he lay there sprawled out face down on the pavement. Pain surged throughout his body as he lost all consciousness. The next thing he knew, he was in a hospital. It took him months to heal from that beat down. He vowed to never use again or to allow anyone or anything to have that much power and control over his life.

CHAPTER 1

Alex Stone awoke to someone pounding on the door and his cell phone ringing at the same time. He tried to get up but his arm was weighed down by this incredible, beautiful, naked female with the complexion of caramel. Her hair was cut close in small waves like an ocean. Her name was Tomorrow. She had a perfect shape with a small waist. Stone rubbed her hair with his free hand while whispering in her ear, "Wake up and piss baby, the world is on fire."

She awakened giving him a little smile. Her eyes were the color of coffee with plenty of cream. She started pecking at his chest with small kisses while her hand probed down his hard frame seeking his member. Stone felt himself becoming aroused, feeling the warmth of her breath on his body. Stone's mind wandered back to him watching her walk naked from the hot tub to the bed last night. Damn! I love the way she walks, he thought to himself. She stood 5'9", with everything in the right place. "Baby, we're being summoned by the phone and the door," said Stone, while standing and wrapping a sheet around his naked 6'1" medium frame, with muscles rippling from his stomach ,arms, and legs.

Tomorrow winced from the cold chill of the air conditioner that moved across her now exposed body. She grabbed the remaining sheet that was at the foot of the bed. While covering herself, she kept her eyes on Stone's naked behind, she also liked watching him walk, especially naked. "I'm sure it's Carol and Allen", Tomorrow said while Stone looked through the peep hole in the door.

Sure enough it was Carol and Allen. Tomorrow and Carol had been friends since grade school and both shared ownership of one of the most profitable beauty shops in town. The two females often spent time with Stone and Allen, who also just happened to be close friends and combined business owners of a night club, with high priced exotic dancers. It was these two men who had helped the girls on their feet.

Tomorrow and Carol were forever grateful, however, they repaid Stone and Allen the money they borrowed to get the beauty shop started. Now they owned it free and clear. The men admired and loved the independence and business savvy in these women. Tomorrow and Carol told them flat out that they didn't want to beholden to anyone. Stone and Allen couldn't agree with them more because if it didn't make dollars it didn't make sense. That had been three years ago and the girls hadn't looked back since.

Almost dying in that alley had plagued his memory. From that day forth, Alex Stone made some life changing decisions and stuck to them. He purged his body of drugs and now worked out daily. He started working two jobs, and did as much overtime as the jobs would allow him, and he hustled on the side. All the while, saving his bank to invest in something bigger, more prominent, and legit. All of his life Stone had just survived. Now he would live. He took the money he saved and left Detroit, Michigan on a bus with just the clothes on his back. That was ten years ago...

Stone opened the door. Both Carol and Allen walked in with cell phones to their ears. Stone closed the door asking Tomorrow, "Who's on the phone baby?"

Before Tomorrow could respond, Carol answered, "It was us, calling the both of you. We were worried when you didn't answer the hotel phone."

Tomorrow said, "I shut my cell phone off."

"Yeah, I'm just glad to see we were worrying for nothing," replied Carol, who stood there with her hands on her nicely shaped hips. She stood 5'6". Her hair was medium length. She was a light skinned sister with a big ass that made men take more than one look in her direction.

"Why are you so early anyway?" Tomorrow asked, while looking at her watch. "It's only nine o'clock. Check out time isn't it until noon. Is everything Okay?"

Allen chimed in, "Yeah everything is fine."

"Well that being the case, if this hotel isn't on fire, I'm trying to lay back down with the warmth that baby generates," added Stone as he went back over to the bed and climbed in beside Tomorrow. Allen and Carol took to the chairs.

Allen said, "I can see the two of you are grumpy because we interrupted your morning cocktail, huh Stone?"

Stone and Allen joked and made light of most things, but their serious side coupled with their business sense, measured up to the success they now enjoyed.

"Yeah, and I'll bet they been he-ing and she-ing the whole night long," added Carol, as she noticed the clothes that were thrown about the room.

"Guilty as charged," said Stone.

"I'm sure I speak for the both of us when I say, we'll take a plea bargain on that," said Tomorrow while looking into Stone's eyes. Pulling her eyes from Stone, she directed her attention to Carol and Allen saying, "It ain't like you two were next door playing tic tac toe."

"Yeah, you're right about that. My baby Allen was going strong girl, making my toes curl and the whole nine yards until his Niagara wore off," answered Carol.

"Honey, it's not Niagara, It's Viagra," said Allen, feeling a bit embarrassed.

"Well you would have thought it was Niagara the way you had my Juices flowing when you were up and going strong," Carol added with a little smile. Stone and Tomorrow laughed at the two of them.

Carol noticed Tomorrow and Stone were fondling each other under the covers, she reached over and put her hand on Allen's lap close by his jewels. "Well whatever it is, we want some of whatever keeps you two all touchy and feely."

"No enhancers, just let the senses do what they do, sight, smell, taste, touch, and sound, in and out of itself is a big turn on for me. But I'm sure you two didn't come here to get schooled on how we get down. So what's on your mind?"

"Stone, I'm surprised at you. Did you forget? We planned on picking up my older brother at the train station at noon," said Allen. He was close to the same height as Stone, only Allen was a little heavier and he wore he his hair in short brush waves.

"No I didn't forget. You told me he wouldn't be in until noon tomorrow," replied Stone.

"Stone, today is tomorrow. You've been up all night so in your mind's eye it's still yesterday. Afternoon will be in about two hours," Allen explained while holding up two fingers.

Allen was right, Stone thought to himself, lately he felt he had been a bit off his game. Not from lack of knowledge or experience, but more so because he had been spending more of his time with Tomorrow. Stone only had one living relative that he knew of. His father died when he was only eleven years old. Those who he considered his family now were his boy Allen, and he had become increasingly aware how after three years his feelings had grown even more for this caramel beauty that lay naked beside him.

"My fault Allen, that one got by me. Tell you what, breakfast is on me. Will you and Carol go get breakfast while me and my baby shower and get ourselves together? You fly, I'll buy."

"You know me; I'm always up for free food," answered Allen.

As they headed out the door, Tomorrow winked her eye at her friend and said, "We've got two hours , so you can take your time girl, you know what I mean?"

"I ain't hating on you girl. You get yours. It would have been nice to have gotten my paint can stirred up this morning too. Maybe while they're preparing our food I can get Allen to sneak in the restroom and run up in me," replied Carol with a devilish grin on her face. They all laughed as the two left out closing the door heading for breakfast while the other two in the bed began to he and she.

Shortly after breakfast and dropping the girls off, Stone and Allen were on their way to the train station to pick up Allen's brother, Ronnie Calhoun, A.K.A Spook. Ronnie had just did fifteen years in the Jackson Michigan Prison system for manslaughter. He gained the name "Spook" in his early adulthood. Some said it was because he was so dark, that if he stood next to a rock it looked like a cave. But he'd like to think the true meaning behind the name was the fear he instilled in people. Stone, Allen, and Spook all grew up on the streets of Detroit, Michigan. However, Stone and Allen didn't meet until five years after Spook had went to prison. Allen met Stone at a crap game in the back room of some after hours club. Two masked men made an attempt at robbing the place, only to be jumped by Stone and Allen. The rest of the would be victims came to their aide, beating and kicking the mask men. This strange twist of fate caused Stone and Allen to form a loyal friendship that had lasted ten years and counting. They came to know all about each other and made good going into business together. Allen had come to be the brother Stone never had.

Allen talked about Spook from time to time over the years. He wanted help provide his older brother with a fresh start. Spook was a bit rough around the edges before being locked up. Besides, fifteen years in prison would make anyone want to change his lifestyle for the better. At least, you'd think it would.

They met Spook in the train station. The brothers shook hands and embraced. Stone was introduced and did likewise. In the car, the brothers exchanged memories in the front seat while Stone rode in the back. The sound of Tupac filled the car.

"I really thank you for the care package with the money and all while I was locked up all those years lil brother," said Spook.

"Ronnie, you're my blood. Things like that come natural. I got mad love for you man," answered Allen.

"Back at you on the love tip. But Allen, like I told you back at the train station, call me Spook, my man."

"Ronnie, I've been calling you Ronnie all my life. Now you want me to call you that stupid ass street tag?"

"Yeah, I'm your older brother, cant you respect that? I don't want to be known out there by no other names but Spook. I know we both can be pretty argumentative but let me win this one okay?"

"Okay, you can have this one, this time. Check it out, I 'm going to drop Stone off at his car, he's had a rough night. I'm going to line your pockets with some cash and we're going shopping and get you some clothes, jewelry, and any other accessories that you may need. You can call yourself Spook, but you won't have to look like one," retorted Allen.

"Well, I been locked up way too long without some pussy. After this shopping thing, take me some where to find me a woman, so I can get my nuts out of pawn. Feel like I ain't had no pussy, since pussy had me," said Spook.

"I know that's right," said Stone and Allen at the same time.

CHAPTER 2

Stone and Allen's biggest business venture had been the night club they named "Establishment" after gambling at so many other places and hustling on the streets of Detroit. They both decided to stop taking so many chances and move out of "The D". Stone moved to Battle Creek. It was smaller than Detroit, but average for a town. With its cereal and car parts factories, Stone viewed this to be a profitable business venture that him and his mellow could sink their teeth into with the right moves.

After he settled in, he put his friend Allen up on his game. They could make a clean living with minimum risk. So far so good. They developed a small empire in very little time. Business was doing so well, they hired help to run the bar, female dancers, security, and waitresses. The men even took accounting courses so they could keep their own books. They'd seen too many businesses go belly up because someone was cooking the books.

They also owned pool rooms with gambling in hideaway back rooms and a two story apartment building that had twenty rooms that only housed women of ill repute. Stone and Allen were not pimps, nor did they ever claim to be, however, they did provide a safe working environment for the women who got down like that. Stone and Allen's percentage was high but the women didn't have to pay rent, so everyone was okay with that. The rules were simple to all who affiliated within their circles; No drugs and no stealing from any customers, because this would bring about the heat, and make a dissatisfied customer.

If a person was pleased with the service that you provided, they would spend more money with you than you could take from them. So far, Stone and Allen had been flying below the radar of the police and they wanted to keep it that way. If the truth be told, they knew of several police officers that frequented the apartments of ill repute. As long as no one was getting hurt or robbed they seem to live and let live. It wasn't always like that. When Stone and Allen first started this arrangement, they ran into some wrinkles. There were those who used drugs, those who tried to sell drugs, those who stole customers, and some of so called small town popcorn pimps' whores went over to Stone and Allen's stable. After Stone and Allen laid their gangster down, everybody who was somebody respected their gangster. The customers started coming back when word got out the violators had been weeded out. Now, business had never been better. They even hired an older women of ill repute to oversee things at the apartments.

Her name was Dorothy. She was taller than most women and big boned, let her tell it. She had shoulder length hair, huge breasts, big eyes, and would cut you if she thought you opposed a threat to the operation. Also, she didn't mind cussing you out for looking at her sideways. She had some meat on her bones, age hadn't robbed her of her beauty, and she would fight. It was rumored that she would charge at you like a bull. Stone and Allen knew she would be good for this job. They also hired some security personnel to keep out the bad element. Stone and Allen appointed a big field hand of a man to be the overseer of the club. Dwayne had experience running a bar. Dwayne was also from Detroit. He moved because Stone and Allen paid him well.

He was a big man. He stood 6'6", with a barrel chest. He had been a bouncer in many clubs back in "the D". Dwayne wore brush waves and his hands were so huge his fingers looked like polish sausages. He ran a tight ship and was given permissions to hire his own employees to work the bar. It was common knowledge the Dwayne was the number one man. He only answered to Stone and Allen. He had been working for them now for eight and a half years. They were pleased with the workers they had up to this point.

Stone sat in the back at their private table with Tomorrow and Carol listening to the sounds of Usher. The girls looked beautiful in their low cut, high profile dresses. Stone was dressed in a white Italian suit, with Italian black soft leather shoes. He excused himself from the girls and went towards the bar to speak with Dwayne. Stone wore his hair in a pony tail. He had a medium complexion and women in the bar took notice as he made his way to the bar. Stone was speaking to Dwayne when Allen and Spook entered the club.

Allen had dark skin but not as dark as Spook. Allen also wore a suit, beige silk with the double splits in the back. Spook just wore a pressed shirt and creased pants to show more of his bulky frame. Both men carried their long coats over their arms. Spook towered over his younger brother at 6'8". He was also wide at the chest and shoulders. They went over to where the girls sat and Allen introduced Spook to Carol and Tomorrow. Stone witnessed Tomorrow standing up and throwing her drink in the face of Spook while making his way to their table.

Allen put his hand on his brother's shoulder trying to stop him from confronting Tomorrow. Carol fished around in her purse and now held a small. 25 semi- automatic under the table pointed in the direction of Spook. Allen knew this could get real ugly, real quick. He also knew Tomorrow well enough to know that she wouldn't have done such a thing unless provoked. The same could not be said for Spook. Stone had made his way to Tomorrow's side to access the threat. She was standing with her hands on her hips, mad, and very heated. Stone could always tell when his baby was angry because her nostrils would open and close like a bull. Spook shoved Allen's hand off his shoulder.

Carol still had the .25 auto pointed directly at Spook. She didn't want to shoot him but she would put a few hot ones in him if he advanced toward her girl. No one but Allen even noticed she had the gun.

"Spook, what the hell is wrong with you?" shouted Allen much louder than he intended.

"What's wrong with me? I'm the one standing here with her drink on my face; she's the one who's trippin'," shouted Spook. Spit flew from his mouth and the veins in his neck and forehead began swelling.

Stone kept his eyes trained on this big man. He wanted so much to knock Spook's grill out, but he'd wait to hear her side of the story. "Tomorrow!" was all Stone said while never taking his eyes off Spook.

Tomorrow knew Stone wanted to hear what she had to say. He had schooled her that even in a bad situation to stay calm and if you have to check someone, speak your mind and do it intelligently. She took a deep breath and let it out before speaking. "Allen had just introduced us to his brother here, Spoon, Spook, or whatever his name is. Anyway, after he sat down he tried reaching between my legs under the table." She rolled her big beautiful eyes at Spook although she desperately wanted to spit in his face.

Two of the bouncers came to see what was going on. Stone waved them away. At the same time Allen said to Spook, "We run a respectable business here. You're my brother and I love you but, you can't be disrespecting my close friend and clowning in our place of business. I can't and won't tolerate such behavior. You've embarrassed me here tonight."

Spook looked into his little brother's eyes and saw the disgust on his face. Spook didn't want his brother upset. Plus, whatever Allen was doing, it was working for him. Allen had money. The last thing Spook wanted to do was to disrupt his cash flow. His brother was making money and staying out of trouble. Spook would see to it that it stayed that way. He decided to clean up the situation. Everyone saw the tension drain from his face.

Spook gestured to the whole table, "Look, I apologize. I guess the drinks are getting to me. Tomorrow, I truly apologize to you. I'll respect the business and all of you."

Stone weighed his words carefully. His voice was cold as he warned, "Allen is being kind because you're his brother. Allen is also my best friend, because of that, I too will be kind. You didn't know she's with me so I won't take it personal. But, I will pay you the compliment of being blunt, with all due respect to you. If something like this happens again, nothing nice will become of it." Stone looked up into Spook's eyes. Even though Spook towered over him and was afraid of no man, there was something about Stone that made him bear caution.

Spook thought, "Maybe some other time I'll try him and see what he's really made of." Out loud he said, "Relax, I was just trying to have some fun and got carried away. No harm was intended." He held both of his palms out towards Stone. An uncomfortable silence hung in the air.

"Tomorrow you okay with that?" asked Stone.

"What's done is done. Let's not let it ruin our night," answered Tomorrow.

"So we are good?" Stone asked Spook as he and Tomorrow took their seats.

Spook sat down and wiped his face with a napkin, "Yeah, everything is tight."

Carol put away the gun and broke the ice saying, "I'm glad that's settled girl. I got to pay that rest room some attention. Come on girl lets go freshen up." She grabbed Tomorrow's hand and lead the way to the rest room.

Things settled down and everyone seemed to enjoy themselves. A short time later, Stone and Tomorrow said their goodbyes. They let Carol and Allen know they were going back to the same hotel because they both had been drinking and did not want to drive. Outside the club, Tomorrow asked, "Why not spend more time at your place or mine?"

Stone replied, "Because I like room service."

"Well, Stone baby, I'll give you all the room service you want."

"Okay. I'll get the room and you service me."

They kissed in the back seat of the cab. Then she laid her head on his shoulder as the cab made its way through the slushy streets. Tomorrow was deep in thought. She knew Stone saw other women. They had never made a commitment to each other. But whenever they were together, the sparks flew! She often wanted to request for them to settle down and get married. Then, as always, she dismissed the entire idea. "Who knows? Maybe someday he'll ask me," she thought to herself, "but tonight, he's all mine." She smiled from ear to ear as the cab pulled into the hotel's parking lot.

Back at the club, Allen let the workers know Spook was his brother. Spook loosened up and danced with all who would dance. However, he was very interested with one of the strip tease dancers he had been stalking all night. Her name was Lisa. She was a very nice looking woman. She was shaped like an hour glass. She was half white and half black, with green eyes and stood 5'7". They went to the table Carol and Allen occupied. Allen and Carol had known her for some time. Lisa was like most of the girls in the business. It was a job and it paid the bills. Besides, she loved dancing and flirting with men.

She hoped to someday get Stone to bed her. The itch she had for Stone just wouldn't go away and she needed him to scratch it. She never had him, but wanted him bad. She saw him leave with that bitch they call Tomorrow.

The four of them sat there enjoying themselves, talking and laughing. "Hey Allen," said Spook, "Why does your boy Stone talk so proper? I'm sure he wasn't talking that way in Detroit."

"Yeah, well, you could learn something from Stone. He's a pretty smart guy. In fact, if the truth be told, we learn from each other," answered Allen.

"Well, why don't we just all line up to kiss his ass?" said Spook downing another drink.

"You know me better than that, don't hate, congratulate. Me and Stone have put money in your pockets and you now have your very own car. And a house that you can call your home. You don't want for nothing and all you can do is complain?"

"Nah, I really do appreciate all that both of you have done. I'm just saying, why that nigga talk so proper?"

The girls looked at Spook like he had two heads. Allen said, "What I can tell you is he told me that the two most important books are the Bible first and then the dictionary. You and I were also raised up to believe in God. Don't get me wrong, me or Stone don't go around hitting people over the head with the Bible, but we do have strong beliefs in it. No one is without sin, and I'm sure none of us will make angel status. As for the dictionary, I try to look up at least two words a day to improve my vocabulary. Stone inspired me to do that. The people that we do business with... it's almost a must. Words are power when understood and placed in the right order. So you see big brother, you can't just play the part. You must know and understand the esoteric language the people with big money and power speak. There is nothing wrong with a person trying to better himself."

Lisa had started to get wet between her legs just hearing Allen speak about Stone. Stone and Allen both knew Lisa was hot for Stone. She had made some advances but Stone had rejected every one. Not because he wasn't attracted to her, but more so because the timing seemed to always be wrong. Stone and Allen both had helped her out when she needed an outstanding bill paid from time to time.

"I think it's sexy when a man has more upstairs then down," added Lisa with a little giggle.

"Yeah, who asked you anyway!" barked Spook. He wanted to slap her.

The way Spook acted and spoke to Lisa made Carol feel a bit uncomfortable. "Baby, it's getting late. If you want some of this, you better get me out of here while I'm still awake with some energy. It's my turn to open up the shop tomorrow," said Carol. She placed Allen's hand under the table between her opened legs.

Allen felt the heat coming from the hairy bush she had guided him to. "Lisa can we give you a ride anywhere?" asked Carol.

"Nah girl, I'm straight, thanks anyway," Lisa said moving closer to Spook.

"Okay, baby let's move," Allen said, taking Carol's hand. Carol noticed Allen's pants was poking out, and thought, maybe just maybe he'd do her without the aid of any enhancers tonight. After Allen helped Carol with her coat, he turned to Spook and asked, "You gonna be alright man?"

"I'm your big brother. Hell yeah I'm ah be alright,"

"Well keep your cell phone on. I'll get back at you tomorrow big brother."

Spook nodded his head and turned his attention back to Lisa. What Lisa didn't know was before Spook had gone to prison for manslaughter he was one of the most brutal pimps that Detroit had given birth too. He thought to himself, "She will be my special treat tonight."

Lisa had drank more than she had intended, plus the weed she and Spook had smoked added to it. She didn't want to but Spook had insisted that she turn him on to someone who he could cop some weed. They drove around smoking and drinking in the car Allen had bought Spook earlier.

Now, they climbed the steps to her apartment. Her head was spinning so fast she found it hard to get the key in the lock. Once they were inside, she told him to wait while she went to the rest room and freshened up. Spook sat on the coach and fired up a fat blunt. The smoke from it was thick and pungent. It moved about the room like a transparent serpent.

Lisa returned from the rest room. "Spook baby, I'm not feeling too well. I've been in there throwing up. Would you put that blunt out? I have a seventeen year old who is spending the night at his friends. I don't want Jason coming home to a house that smells like weed. I smoke it, but the last thing I want to do is encourage him to use a drug of any kind."

"Shut up bitch! You're fucking up my high, and you're fucking with my addiction. Show me your bedroom," said Spook while exhaling a mouth full of smoke in her face.

"Excuse me!" said Lisa. Her eyes started to sting from the weed smoke. Before she saw it coming, Spook punched her in her stomach causing her to expel all of her stomach contents on the rug. She fell to the floor and passed out in her own vomit.

When she awakened the last piece of her clothing was being taken off. The man straddled her and started slapping her. He beat her until she welcomed the darkness that took over her. He placed himself inside thinking how good the pussy felt. He increased his tempo. A few moments later, he turned her unconscious form over and forcefully entered Lisa from the rear.

28

CHAPTER 3

The next morning, one of Carol's friends called to tell her how Lisa was in the hospital and they didn't think she would make it. Carol called Tomorrow and Allen with the bad news. Allen called Stone. Allen and Stone made their way through the hospital halls to the hospital emergency room. Tomorrow and Carol were already there, hugging and talking to some older woman and a teenage boy. Carol introduced them to Lisa's mother and son. The small group did what they could to comfort them, but it was to no avail. Stone thought to himself, "What could a person do or say to ease the hurt of loved ones in a situation like this? Nothing much. Just try to be there the best you can when they need you."

The mother was crying her eyes out, but the son looked very distant, extremely detached to his surroundings, there was a blank stare in his eyes. This would probably scar Jason mentally for the rest of his life.

Two men wearing cheap suits and ties that looked like they were made from the curtains off someone's window approached. Stone and Allen said it at the same time, "Cops."

They flashed their badges. The younger of the two was going bald and the other was completely white headed, They introduced themselves with some names no one would remember and asked everyone questions concerning Lisa.

They asked the general questions like, "Did she have enemies? Does she have a boyfriend or husband, and if so are they the jealous type? Does she do drugs? Does she owe anyone on the streets money?" The more questions they asked the more racist they sounded. Some of the question was borderline, yet, they were still condescending.

The older of the two pulled Stone and Allen off to the side, away from Lisa 's family, "Since she was employed at your place of business we might have more questions later. By the way, her house was trashed, some money and a .32 caliber gun was taken. Whoever raped and beat her poured bleach in her vagina, probably with hopes of destroying any D.N.A.. The Captain says this one is top priority. I hope whatever we find doesn't lead us to you two. Were familiar with your reputation, so far, you've been able to keep it clean.

I guess what I'm saying is if either of you know anything or should find out anything, you really need to share it with me. Hell, even if you could make it go away I'd be happy, the last thing we all don't need is big waves in our small town. Now, is there anything you know?"

Allen and Stone both shook their heads no. Just then, the doctor came in and announced Lisa would make it. "She suffered some broken bones, Internal bleeding, but she will heal given some time. The bad news is she's is in a coma. She could come out of it in ten minutes or ten years. There's just no way to know right now. The immediate family can see her but only for a short while."

The mother stopped crying and seemed to have a glimmer of hope in her eyes. She said, "I know you two are good men. Lisa told me how you've helped her with bills when Jason's father went to prison. I am so grateful." Then she turned to the police. "I pray you find the monster that did this to my baby. Now I'm going to my daughter's side. Please let me know the minute you find something out." Then she took her grandson Jason's hand and walked out of the emergency room with the doctor.

The detectives headed for the door, the one with the white hair turned back, then said , "We'll be in touch." He laid his card on the table besides the hospital magazines, then left with his partner.

"That no good Spook!" shouted Carol. Allen held his forefinger up to his lip to quiet Carol down. The men ushered the women out to Carol's car since it was the closest to the emergency room door. All four got inside the car. "Allen, we all know damn well Spook was with Lisa last night."

"That doesn't mean that Spook did it", added Allen.

"Carol didn't say he did it, but I'm sure we were all thinking it," Tomorrow said coming to her girl's defense.

"He was with her last night. That's a fact. However, to keep it on the up and up, we can't convict Spook without any evidence. That's the way the prosecutors and Judges dog us in a courthouse. They did a rape kit on her. If it comes back positive with samples of Spook, then we'll know for sure," concluded Stone.

Allen said, "I tried calling him but I'm not getting an answer."

"Listen, Allen and I need to hit the streets and put our ears to the ground. Hopefully, we'll catch up to Spook," said Stone. "I'll call you later."

The girls agreed that for that moment this would probably be the best course of action. They kissed the girls and went to Allen's house. From what Allen could tell, Spook had not been back there. He looked in Spook's bedroom, the bed had not been slept in. As far as they knew, Spook didn't know anyone in Battle Creek. Or did he?

They decided to split up and cover more ground by checking the gambling joints and some local bars, plus their very own bar, but still no Spook. After a few hours, Stone called Allen, who hadn't had any luck in finding his brother. Allen was turning in early. Maybe his brother would show up at home. Someone was calling on Stone's other line. He asked Allen to hold on.

"Hello. Hi baby," it was Tomorrow sweet voice.

"Hey Bee Spit," said Stone. Bee Spit was the pet name he'd given her. The first time he called her that she was offended. He explained that it was bee spit and pollen that made honey. It was his strange way of calling her honey, now she loved that pet name.

"What are you doing?" asked Tomorrow.

"Been in this car for some time going from place to place trying to help Allen find his brother. Why? What's up with you?"

"I was just calling to let you know that I'll be staying up here at the hospital with Carol and Lisa's mother for tonight. Jason went back to his friend's house. His mother said Jason could stay the night and go to school with her son tomorrow."

"That's nice of you and Carol to stay and comfort her. You let me know if there is anything I can do. I mean that okay?"

"Okay and baby I know you mean it. I'll let her know you said so."

"I'll call you when I get up baby. I have Allen on the other line."

Allen has you on hold too. Carol Is speaking to him as we speak. She's sitting right by me. We just wanted to let you guys know that we'd be staying up here. There have been any changes in Lisa's condition. I really should get back to her bedside. They finally allowed us in after her mother put up a fuss."

"Alright, you stay sweet my bee spit."

"Goodbye you sexy man."

The line disconnected and shortly Allen returned. Both men agreed to meet at Stone's the following day. Stone made it home feeling a little tired, but not really sleepy. He thought out loud, "Lately the only time I've been here is when I shave, bathe, change clothes, and put money in the safe."

He felt the need for female company so he called Delsena. They had been messing around almost as long as him and Tomorrow. Nothing serious, they just brought each other sexual comforts when the other was in need. However, she had always wanted more out of the relationship .

Stone was the only man in her life that she allowed to touch her in that way. She was a dark skinned beauty, Long hair, high cheek bones, C-sized breasts and a nice sculptured ass, and stood six feet even with long legs. He thought to himself, "Okay, who am I kidding, it is serious."

They both came from his steamy hot shower and went straight to his king sized bed. Luther Vandross was playing softly. The bedroom was predominately white and gold, right down to the bedside lamps, along with white bed covers and satin sheets. Still dripping wet she laid on her back as he climbed on top of her. They kissed and Stone slid his tongue down her neck to her breast. They felt like ripened fruit. The candle light shined a low level glow that gave their naked bodies a gleam as flesh touched flesh. Stone softly nibbled and sucked on her breast, giving each one the attention they deserved. Delsena's breathing became louder as she took in breaths of air through her clenched teeth.

"Oh baby", was her reply.

Now Stone made his way south, sliding his tongue down past her naval. Licking and jetting his tongue in out of her love tunnel, while reaching up with his hands he gently squeezed her nipples with his fingers while holding her clit between his lips. Thumbing it with the tip of his tongue like a cat licks milk.

"Oh baby, oh baby, baby, baby, baby!" cooed Delsena. She arched her back, allowing her climax to dominate her, while holding his head at the very spot that made her surrender. She tried to turn Stone over. She badly wanted to taste him now.

Stone stopped her saying, "I'm going to service you tonight baby."

She smiled up at him and pulled him up to her kissing him and tasting him and her juices on his mouth. She reached down and guided his already hard member inside her bushy mound of pleasure. He felt the warmth and moisture as she engulfed his wand and matched his tempo. Stone would only give her half of him, going so far in then pulling back. He Knew this increased her desire for him even more. Delsena grabbed his rear, plunging him farther and harder within her.

"Yes baby, that's nice, you want it all baby?"

"Oh yes baby, you make me feel so good," breathed Delsena.

"Take me baby. Take all of this," said Stone as he increased the tempo even faster, stabbing harder and deeper.

"Yes, yes, yes, oh, oh, oooh baby , oh ooooh , Sto, Sto, Stone baby its yours," cried Delsena, with tears of joy.

Opening her legs wide as she could while pointing them up at the ceiling she increased as her juices flowed. She couldn't seem to stop cumming. The flood gates were opened. He had the key to her kingdom and it was deep in her lock.

CHAPTER 4

"Do you remember me? I was here last night or this morning. It depends on how you look at it. I bought a little something from your boys," said the tall dark figure.

"Yeah, I remember you. You were with that fine ass broad," answered the crack head working the door. "You think you could give me a taste when you cop? It's been a while since I've had a bump."

"I'm her for some weed like I bought last night my man."

Well they sell both. Look out for me and I'll get you back. I swear," said the door man.

"We'll see. Now can I take care of my business, or do I have to buy from someone else?" The tall dark man was irritated.

"Right this way my man."

The door man lead him into the house. Three men were seated at a table playing dominoes and drinking. It was plain to see they were strapped to the gills. Each man was young and had saggin' pants down around their butts. Their underwear showed just like the guns. Both were meant to be seen. This was the neighborhood's low rent housing. Plenty of drugs and troubles came with it. The three men looked up.

" Hey Q! You got a custo," said the door man.

"You stupid ass crack head. You know the drill. Ask that motherfucker what he wants. Can't you see I'm playing bones and taking these nigga's money?" shouted Q.

The tall dark man was swift. He pulled his gun, pointed it at the three, grabbed the door man by his collar, and slung him at the table. Dominoes and the men's drinks went crashing to the floor. The young men looked at this unknown man in disbelief. The door man laid on the floor while the others backed against the wall with hands held high.

"What the fuck?" said the door man as he tried to regain his footing.

"What the fuck is this? A jack?" asked one of the young men.

"Shut up!" said the tall dark man moving closer, still pointing his gun at them. "Slowly, and I do mean slowly, toss your guns over here on the floor," he demanded.

The men thought and weighed their chances. His gun was already out. They'd be shot before they could pull theirs. They unwillingly did what he said. One of the guns was big and pretty, if a gun could be called such. It was a Desert Eagle. He checked the clip. It was fully loaded. He put the clip back in and put the small .32 caliber in his pocket. Now he pointed the long deadly Eagle in their direction.

"Who is the head man in charge of this show?" asked the tall dark man.

"What you want motherfucker? A job? I'm the man with the big nuts," said Q.

Without hesitation the dark man walked up to Q and shot him point blank range in the head. Q was dead before he hit the floor. Blood, brain matter, and pieces of bone peppered the remaining men as they watched in horror, shock, and disbelief.

"Now who's in charge?" shouted the dark man.

"You are!" yelled the other young men.

Spook smiled. He replayed the event that led up to this point inside his head. Once he knocked out Lisa, Spook had went through her house looking for whatever he could find. The bankroll his brother had given him was still in his room. It wasn't much, a little over five grand, but he sure could use it now. Three hundred seventy dollars was in her purse and six hundred more was found in the bedside table along with a .32 revolver hand gun. Before he left, he checked her breathing to make sure that she was still alive. He'd never seen a bitch drop to the floor and be out like a light so quick.

Spook snapped back to reality. He focused on the present and the three men before him. He made them a proposal, work with him, have fun while doing it, or die here and now. Spook was forty years old and still in good shape. The men before him were in the age ranges of twenty-five, to thirty. He viewed them to be easy to lead. All they needed was an alpha male to rule the pack.

The door opened to his right. Spook shifted his attention and gun in that direction. A female, barely dressed in panties and bra exited the bedroom. She saw Q's body on the floor with half of his head attached.

This was what the three men needed, a slight distraction. They saw their chance. One ran and dived behind some furniture. The other two rushed Spook. Spook tore his attention from the woman, but he was too late. The two men were all over him like a cheap suit. The gun was knocked from Spook's hand. They knocked down everything they came in to contact with, including the female. She gave a little scream as she hit the floor hard. Her mind was still processing what she was witnessing. The dope dealers were in mortal combat with some big dark man.

***

Stone and Allen went over the books at their club "Establishment". The night club seemed to be in order. Dwayne seemed to worth his weight in gold.

"I need you to keep your ear to the streets for me Dwayne," asked Allen.

"Sure, not a problem, anything in particular?"

"If you see or hear anything about my brother, let me or Stone know."

"Alright, I'll put someone on it. I'll call you the minute I know something," said Dewayne.

Allen and Stone went to the back room where a dice game was in progress. There were several tables off to the side where they played poker. They greeted the men, gambled for a while, and then left. Snow crunched under their feet as they made their way to their cars. It was a bitter cold afternoon and both men wore long coats.

Today they had chose to ride in the twin Fleetwood Cadillac's. Allen was canary yellow, and Stone's was royal blue. These were part of their vintage collection of the few classic s they owned. Not to mention, they both had several up to date sport cars, and each had an S.U.V.. They pulled in the parking lot of "Mirrors", the girl's beauty shop. Eight female employees who worked there. When the men entered, all eyes were on them. The girls knew these men were exclusively Carol's and Tomorrow's. The girls gave the men a wave of the hand and a smile. When a chair became open, the girls groomed them the way Allen and Stone always liked.

The main topic of conversation was Lisa. There still had not been any changes in her condition. The girls planned to go back up to the hospital later that night. Carol and Allen had disappeared. Tomorrow grabbed Stones hand and led him to the back door that entered into her house that was connected to the shop. Now with them both in her bedroom she hugged and kissed him and then began to unzip his pants.

"I want you inside me now," she said with urgency, "In case I don't get to see you tonight."

She was wearing jeans and was out of those before she finished her sentence. Looking at the mound between her legs, made him hard as prison steal. She pushed him gently on his back and took his erect staff in her mouth. She was excited and sucking too fast. Stone took hold of her head in both of his hands, slowing her down so that she went up and down in even strokes.

"Yeah, just like that baby," breathed Stone.

He reached down and began to rub her nipples in a circular motion. She began to feel moisture between her thighs. Stone now felt she was on point. He wanted to explode right here and now, but held back for as long as he could. Tomorrow was working with it and then she did something that just took over the edge. She hummed with him fully in her mouth. The feeling was overwhelming. Stone couldn't do nothing but let go of her head and grip the sheets. He held on like he was on a roller coaster. He gave a grunt as he spewed his sperm. She swallowed most and allowed the remaining to run on her body. Then she rolled over on her back and rubbed it on her body as if it was lotion. Both were breathing hard.

"Damn baby," breathed Stone, "That was good as usual, but with a kick! Where did you learn the humming thing? That vibration thing you did with your mouth was out cold."

"This girl, I won't mention any names, whose hair I did earlier said she does that to her man and it drives him crazy," answered Tomorrow, "Did you like it?"

"Baby, I enjoyed it more then I can express, it was like my life juices were drained right out of me.

"I couldn't wait to try that on you," she said while rubbing his sperm on her swollen clit. She smiled at him. Stone looked at this beautiful woman and became aroused again. He rolled on top of her.

"Cum inside me and put this fire out," she whispered in a sexy voice. Without hesitation, Stone complied.

***

Both men were trying to hold this big man down and land some blows. Their fists didn't seem to have any effect on this big man. Spook had no use of his hands because each of the men had an arm still tussling to bring Spook under control.

Spook knew if they got the best of him, they would kill him or worse, torture him and then kill him. He summoned all his strength and head butted one in his nose causing him to let go of his muscular arm. The dealer was holding his nose. Falling back and holding his face with blood soaked hands. Spook hit the other with his free hand right on the side of his neck. It sounded like someone biting down on ice. The blow broke his neck. He fell face first, never to move on his own again. Spook was now up on his feet, he turned to see the man with the broken nose being choked by the crack head door man. Spook was surprised to see him attacking the dope dealer. The female was watching with amazement and she had her fingers in her panties. She fingered herself. Was she masturbating while looking at this carnage?

The man being choked was now dead, but the skinny door man still had in him a G.I. Joe death grip. The dead man's eyes bulged out of his head. "Mutha Fucka! You won't be doggin' nobody else out." The door man finally let go of the dead man. Breathing hard he looked up into the long barrel of the gun Spook held on him. Spook had recovered the .45 Desert Eagle.

"Well, my offer still stands. You in, or out?" asked Spook.

The door man was scared speechless of the man with the gun. He had an evil look about him. There were beads of sweat on his forehead but he mustered up enough courage to say, "Hell yeah I'm in. Fuck these muthafuckas. They paid me in dope to watch the door but constantly dogged me out in the front of their friends, making me crawl for dope and kicking my ass just because I smoke crack."

"So what's your name?" asked Spook. His guns were on the man but the girl was in his sight too.

"My name is Derrick, but I'm called Crack Pipe. That's what I go by. Some make fun of the name, but I'm not in denial. I like crack, so I smoke the shit. Call me Crack pipe." Then he asked Spook, "What's your name if you don't mind me asking?"

Spook noticed that the female licking her fingers as if she had eaten some fried chicken or something. The very same fingers she had just pulled out of her panties. She looked Spook up and down. Spook was turned on to see her taste herself. "I understand where you're coming from on the nicknames, call me Spook." He pointed his finger at the woman. "So, what's up with her? What's her story?"

Crack Pipe pointed to his head, making a circular motion. Indicating that she was crazy. "Her porch light is on but no one's home."

"So what's her name?"

"My name is Isis, and you can talk to me," she said still looking at the dead men.

"Okay, so what's the deal with you?" Spook asked with interest.

She turned to look at him with wicked green eyes. She was short and well stacked. Her face was average with a dark complexion and her hair was combed straight to the back with bangs in front. She had a small mole by the corner of her upper lip.

"She's a freak," added Crack Pipe.

"Why don't you shut the fuck up? He was talking to me. I'm a diabolical freak. Get that shit right if you going to tell it," retorted Isis.

"So you're a freak in the bed huh?" inquired Spook.

"Yeah, I'm down for mines. Long as I got a man like yourself to look after me and keep me supplied in the stuff, I'll do whatever is clever. You know what I mean big fella?"

46

Spook tucked the Dessert Eagle in his waist band and asked Crack Pipe, "Can she be trusted?"

"You know they say none of us crack heads can be trusted, but as long as she's supplied she will do what she's told. Oh by the way so will I," said Crack Pipe. He looked like a bag of bones as he gave Spook a smile with some missing teeth.

"You just killed a man. At the same time you helped me out. It's because of that I don't kill you alongside him, so that says a little for you. Now how can I know that I can trust her?"

"Because, I introduced her to these guys two weeks ago. I hated watching her get passed around as a tool of pleasure. I only brought her here because they gave me rocks to bring them a freak. I knew she got high and like to fuck. I thought I would be helping us both out, but I seen the hell they put her through and I knew she should be trying to do something about it." Crack Pipe's voice was full of concern.

"Don't go talking that sob ass shit. I knew what I was getting into. I knew what I was doing. So don't you develop a conscience now Muthafucka. Spook, I'm down for mine and I'm in, if you'll have me," said Isis.

Spook looked at this well shaped female in the small compact frame. She still had her sexy look about her. The hard life of the streets and drugs hadn't rubbed her of that yet. He liked what was in her and loved her I don't give a fuck gangster attitude. Maybe he could use her in more ways than one. "My question still hasn't been answered. Why does Crack Pipe thinks I can trust you?"

She pointed to the guns that Spook had on them and said, "Well, other than me being able to screw your lights out and being a gangster bitch, I know how to use one of those. Plus Crack Pipe knows that you can trust me because, his mother and father are my mother and father. I'm his sister."

CHAPTER 5

Spook, Isis, and Crack Pipe took the dope and money from the house. The money added up to a little over $25,000.00 and it was 1 1/2 kilos of cocaine and 5 ounces of weed. Spook had parked his car at a nearby closed factory. Then they went to a used car lot and brought a van. Crack Pipe and Isis wanted to get high but Spook told them he would issue them some in small amounts after they got the van. Now that was done and they were riding down the snow plowed streets with Spook behind the wheel. The other two were in the back getting high. It was beginning to get dark out and the snow had started to come down in big flakes. Spook pulled in the parking lot of a supermarket and parked far from the entrance as he could get. He shut the van off and gave Crack Pipe some money and a list of things that they would need. He also told him to take his time so he and Isis could get in the mix.

"Okay, just let me get one more hit alright?" said Crack Pipe.

Spook thought to himself that for now, he would give it to him. He would condition him to some discipline in time. Spook gave him a half a rock. It made a hissing sound like an angry snake when put in the hot pipe. The smoke was strong throughout the van. Isis was already laying on her back naked. Crack Pipe opened the door and got out when Spook went to the back of the van with Isis.

He undid his pants and allowed them to drop around his ankles. "Are you ready for this?" Spook asked. He held his dick in his hand. Isis looked at it and liked the size. He was well endowed in that area.

She opened her legs, pushed her fingers in out of her pussy a couple of times saying, "Yeah I'm ready, you ready for this wet and juicy pussy?"

Spook got ready to mount her but when he got within two feet of her; the funk from her pussy assaulted his nose. He balled his face up and with a contorted expression, as if he tasted some spoiled collard greens. His once hard dick had now started to shrink.

"Bitch! Hell naw I ain't ready for that nasty ass shit. Your pussy smells like a Panda cage! Don't you ever put me in any shit like that!" Spook shouted while pointing at her Vagina. "Bitch we going to clean yo ass up first."

Spook went to the window and called Crack Pipe back. He added ten disposable douches to the list for Isis, then told him to hurry back. His plan was to get to a hotel room where they all could get cleaned up before he made any more moves on her or the streets. Isis had heard what he said to Crack Pipe and smiled while melting down another rock on her pipe, inhaling the smoke, loving the sound of the hissing snake and the feeling that came behind it. She put her fingers back in her pussy, and closed her eyes, releasing all the smoke in her lungs she smiled to herself and began getting herself off.

***

The two detectives just left Allen house. His brother Ronnie Calhoun, A.K.A Spook was wanted for questioning in regards to the assault and rape and on Lisa. When Allen asked if there was a warrant out for Spook 's arrest, they told him they needed to talk him. Witnesses had seen him with Lisa.

Later, Allen sat at the table with Stone at one of their after hour gambling joints. Allen told Stone about the detectives. They collected the house money and were having a drink when Allen's phone rang.

"Hello," he said.

"What's up lil bro?" replied the voice on the other end.

"Ronnie! Where the hell are you ?"

"I got me a room. I'm chillin'."

"Man what's going on? The police are looking for you."

"What the hell for this time?"

"Because Lisa was raped and brutally beaten. She's in a coma!"

"Whaaat?!?"

"Yeah, she is in very bad shape," replied Allen.

Spook thought about the punch he had delivered to her. "They don't think I had nothing to do with it, do they?"

"I'm not sure, but people did see you leave with her. Right now there's no warrant. But the detectives said you're a person of interest and they would like to talk to you."

"Well they will have to wait until tomorrow. Right now I'm getting ready to get my freak on," said Spook with excitement in his voice.

"Either meet me somewhere in a couple of hours or I can come where you're at, so we can make some sense out of the whole thing. Man I need to know. Tell me that it wasn't you."

"You should know me better than that. I'm smart enough to know that three people can keep a secret if two are dead. I don't leave witnesses. Look, I was just calling to check on you and let you know that I'm alright. You're fucking with my addiction with this police shit. I'll get at you when I'm finished with my business. Right now I'm unwinding and relaxed."

"Listen Ronnie this ... "

"Spook, call me Spook!" Spook interrupted him.

"Okay, then listen Spook. This is serious shit and I'm worried about you man. I was hoping that we could go into business together and get paid together. But Spook, you're doing the same stuff that got you caught up before."

"First of all you ain't my parents. I maxed out on my prison sentence, so I don't have no parole officer to report to. So that only leaves one person for me to answer to and that is I. I appreciate your concern, but your worries are misplaced. I didn't do it," Spook barked.

"I'm just trying to look out for you man."

"And I really do appreciate it. I love you lil bro. I'll get a hold of you later. It's not like the world is coming to an end."

"At least let me give you the number the detectives left to call. I love you too. I'd rather see you talk to them on your own terms then for them to gun you down saying their life was threatened by you," pleaded Allen.

"Again, it won't be now. I got to go. I'll pop back at you later."

"Wait Spook!" shouted Allen, but Spook had hung up.

Allen looked over at Stone with the cell phone still to his ear. Stone had heard most of the conversation from Allen's end. His friend looked disappointed as he attempted to call his brother back.

"Spook?" Stone asked.

"Yeah, he's is just as a stubborn as he's always been. I just hope my brother ain't too far gone. I know he doesn't have it all when it comes to good sense, but he is my brother and I love him. He's been through a lot. I just want to be there for him."

"Yeah I can relate, blood is thicker than mud. Allen, you know that I look at you as my family and I will stand by your decision. Now, if Spook's engine is running but no one is behind the wheel, we can expect anything. I won't stand for him hurting you, our people, or destroying everything we've worked so hard for." Stone made it clear.

"I know. You're right. I will draw the line if it comes to our people and our business."

They left to make their rounds in separate cars. The cold weather wasn't letting up. Both men felt the chill of winter cutting at their exposed skin as they walked to the apartment building.

The women could see them from the window. Before the men could open the door with the key, the security buzzed them in. Stone and Allen spoke to the security men then walked down the hall. A few of the women opened their doors trying to get the men to come inside their rooms. From time to time both of them had taken them up on their offers but tonight neither accepted. Dorothy, the Madame of the operation, opened her door which was at the end of the hall on the ground floor.

"Hey fellas," said Dorothy looking the men up and down. "Y'all come on in and get some heat. Its cold out there. My nipples get hard just thinking about it."

The men followed her through the door, watching her voluptuous ass as she switched it through her apartment. They all sat at her dining room table like usual.

"So is everything alright?" asked Stone.

"Nothing I can't handle. We had a trick try to take some pussy from of the girls earlier, and no one was harmed. The trick ended up out there in the snow head first. I don't play that shit," she said.

"I'm glad It all turned out okay," added Allen.

"Oh yeah, the satellite people will be here tomorrow to install the dish for the building," Stone informed her.

"Good, the girls will be pleased. I know y'all didn't come all the way over here to talk about satellite dishes. Tell me what's on your minds." She walked over to a big cabinet. Her gown was see through and she purposely bent over so the men would see the spread of her ass. Dorothy felt the men's eyes on her.

"Business is picking up," Dorothy said. She handed Allen a shoe box full of currency. Allen removed and counted the bills and transferred them to a small duffel bag. The men stood to leave. They were almost to the door when Dorothy said, "Say when is one of y'all one gone give me some dick?"

Both men knew that Dorothy would not hold you up. She said whatever was on her mind. She didn't look bad and was worthy of some dick. But they knew she was dangerous. If any man ever put good dick to her, he'd better marry her because she was destined to be a fatal attraction. Allen and Stone had joked at times how they didn't want Dorothy to cut their nuts off. Both men were in agreement to never stick their wicks into her wax.

Stone decided to stroke her ego and said, "If we ever dip our dicks in that good snapping pussy of yours that we keep hearing about, Allen or I will want to keep you. Which in turn will make me or him jealous of the other and that would end me and his friendship. Now you don't want that do you?"

Allen said, "Besides, I heard it's so good that men will walk through a jungle with a pork chop suit on just to smell it. Hell I'm jealous already."

Dorothy blushed with a big smile. It felt good to her to be complemented by men of their caliber. They didn't know it but just hearing about her own pussy made her wet between the legs.

"Both of y'all could talk sweetness out of a gingerbread cake. And y'all full of it too. I love you both anyway."

They kissed her on the cheek. She grabbed both of their asses before they could respond then she closed the door. Dorothy locked her door and went to her bedroom, opened up her bedside table and pulled out a brand new pack of batteries and her vibrator.

The next morning the men woke up well rested. They made good on their promise to the girls and took them to the hospital to see Lisa. Everyone was happy to hear that Lisa's wounds had started to heal even if she was still in a coma. Her mom and son were there. Jason still had that detached look about him. Stone couldn't even begin to imagine what something like this does to a seventeen year old.

Lisa's mother seemed to read Stone's mind and said, "He'll pull through if the Lord is willing."

Stone thought about his mother. He hadn't visited her for months. He often sent her money and checked on her regularly. His father died when he was eleven years old. He missed his father, a hard worker that spent a lot of time with Stone. While leaving the hospital, Stone asked everyone If they'd like to go shopping and visit his mother In Detroit. They would be back by late night.

Allen was all for it, and the girls just couldn't resist. They dropped the girls off so they could regroup, make sure their shop was in good running order, and gassed up Allen's S.U.V.. The four of them hit the highway, listening to the sounds of Avant. The countryside was like a blanket of snow as far as the eyes could see. The ride down I-94 East had a certain type of relaxing and calming effect.

They arrived safely at Mother Pearl's. She fixed them a good chicken dinner with sweet potato pie for dessert. They were enjoying their food, talking a little and catching each up to what was going on in their lives. Then Mother Pearl asked, "So when are you children going to get married?"

The whole table was blindsided by the question. All four were befuddled. Silence hung over the table. Everyone had stopped in mid-motion. Stone was in the process of taking a drink. The liquid wasn't all the way down when he began to laugh, causing it to come back up. He managed to turn his head away from the table. Everyone, including mother Pearl who patted her son on the back, got a laugh. Finally the laughter died down.

"No really, when?" asked Mother Pearl seriously.

No one answered the question. All of them helped clean up after dinner. Then they went shopping at several malls. The men bought gifts for everyone. Carol and Tomorrow bought Mother Pearl a few things too. Mother Pearl tried to refuse all the gifts, but just like she did them on the food, they wouldn't hear of it. Soon they were tired and it was getting late, so they took Mother Pearl home. She thanked them all, gave kisses, told them not to be strangers, and welcomed them to drop by anytime.

Stone walked his mother to the door and carried her bags in the house. He was compelled to hug and kiss this woman he loved with all of his heart.

"Son, I really enjoyed myself. Thank you for being a wonderful son, all the nice gifts, the money you send, and this nice house," she said.

"Momma, we all thank you for such a wonderful meal, and I personally thank you for being a caring and lovable mother. There is no need to thank me. You gave me life. I could never repay you for that. I was missing you and wanted us to spend some time together. I love you momma."

"That's sweet of you. May the Lord Bless you. I love you too son. I meant what I said earlier about settling down, getting married, and making me some grandbabies. I like your girl. I can tell she loves you. I can see it in her eyes when she looks at you and you two look so good together."

"I just don't know yet momma. I guess a part of me knows what you say is true."

"And the other part?"

"The other part of me still wants to play," answered Stone.

"Son, don't get me wrong, you're doing good for yourself. You run a successful business and all. You even bought me this big expensive house. I'm proud of you and your father would have been proud of you, bless his soul. I can see that she is good for you. I can't live your life for you. When it comes time for God to call your name, only you can die for you. So live life as you see fit, and know I'm telling you this all out of love for you."

"I know momma. I've always valued your words of wisdom. I really care a lot about Tomorrow, but a part of me still likes the streets. I've always been honest with you. I know you'd like to hear the ugly truth over a pretty lie, even when I was an addict, I didn't keep that from you. You were always there for me. You never gave up on me. So I'll keep it real now, I do love her but the streets be calling me and that does include other women."

"Have you told her that you love her? Has she ever told you that she loves you?" asked Mother Pearl.

"She's told me, but I haven't told her. She is aware that I see other women."

"Alex, I won't keep you because your friends are waiting on you out there, but listen to me son. Often what a person is looking for they have already found. As for whatever you're searching for... Have you ever heard the saying that if it walks like a duck, sounds like a duck, and looks like a duck, it's a duck?"

"Of course Momma. Why?"

59

"Well it ain't always a duck, sometimes it's a duck hunter." warned Mother Pearl.

CHAPTER 6

Mother Pearl walked Stone to the door and waved good-bye to them all. The four of them went by a few of Stone's and Allen's old associates houses before heading out to the highway. They also stopped at a bar on 7 mile, on the east side of Detroit. They agreed to have one drink since they still had some traveling to do on the highway back to Battle Creek. The four were seated and enjoying their drinks when two men came over to their table.

"Alex Stone!" said the tall, well dressed man.

All four of them looked at the man. His side kick was short, round, and buffed with bulging muscles. His head looked like it was connected to his body without a neck. There was no doubt how he earned the name "No neck Norman". Stone gave Allen the look. Allen knew it so well.

"Hey Herbert T. What's on your mind?" asked Stone.

"Stone, I thought this was you. What the hell are you doing slumming down here with us common folks? I heard you left "The D" and you doing alright for yourself in some small town. Look at you. You clean up well. I see you got yourself a new set of friends," Herbert T. mused while lusting over the girls.

Herbert T. was one of the dealers Stone bought his drugs from back in the day when he used. In fact, it was Herbert T's boys who busted Stone up and left him in that alley years ago.

"Yeah, these are my good friends. What can I do for you?" asked Stone, with raised eye brows. He didn't bother to introduce anyone.

"I was just coming over to say hello and ask you to come and work for me now that you're all cleaned up. I always knew you were smart and had a good head for business. We can make lots of money together with whatever hustle you got going and my drugs. You don't use that shit anymore, right?"

"Nah, I'm clean. Thanks for the offer but I'm good with the partner I already have. I'm doing my own thing now. Besides, I have no dealings whatsoever with drugs," said Stone.

Allen kept an eye on No Neck. The girls saw where this could lead. Everyone felt tension in the air. Carol hated that she didn't bring her small handgun.

"That wasn't a request Stony boy!" barked Herbert T.

"Look Herbert T., I don't owe anything so remove yourself out from in front of me."

"Fuck you bitch ass nigga! You talking that high powered shit. Are you prepared to back it up mutha fucka?" added No Neck Norman.

Stone played it cool. "Don't you have enough intellect to talk without such a foul and vulgar mouth? Can't you see ladies are present? Do you kiss your mother with that nasty mouth?"

Allen decided to jump in, "Why don't you gentlemen just let this go and let me buy you both a drink?"

"Bitch, when I want your opinion I'll beat it out of you!" shouted No Neck.

"Such anger and hostility. Your friend here is persistent with this primitive linguistic form of communication," said Stone as he shook his head.

Herbert T. didn't really understand what the hell Stone just said, but he felt it was a put down. He had very little education. It really pissed him off to have this once upon a time dope fiend out talk him. You could see the veins swelling in his forehead. Herbert T. was six feet even. He wore a mini afro, a goat-tee, and he was a bit overweight. The extra weight could be seen in his fat cheeks.

"Why don't you thugs just leave us alone?" said Tomorrow, wanting these two men to just go away.

"Yeah what she said," added Carol.

"Well, well, looks like the skirts got more nuts and guts then the so called men at this table. Why don't you ladies come with me and No Neck here and see what real men taste like?"

"Well that rules you both out," retorted Carol.

"Why would that rule us out, Sweet Cheeks?" asked Herbert T.

"Because a real man wouldn't be asking such a stupid question. I would jump over ten just like you to get one of him," said Tomorrow pointing at Stone.

This hit Herbert T. hard. He was enraged. He wasn't use to females talking to him in such a way. "You once a month bleeding, cum burping bitch. Who the fuck do you think you're talking to? Don't you know I'll break this foot off in yo ass?" Herbert T. drew back his hand.

That was a big mistake. Stone sprung from his sitting position, blocking Herbert T's hand in flight. He gave a stiff elbow to Herbert T's face. Herbert T. back paddled as if he were in water. Stone came around the table following through with lefts and rights.

No Neck lunged for Allen over the table. The girls moved away from the table, giving Allen room to maneuver. Drinks, candles, and ashtrays went to the floor. Allen simply moved to the side letting No Neck Norman over extend himself. Allen stood and punched him on the back of his head. No Neck's weight took him over the table.

Screaming and Shouting could be heard among the small crowd. People were trying to make their way to an exit, any exit. Others loved to see me a good fight and stood around to watch. Herbert T. stumbled and almost fell over a chair. He picked it up and threw it at Stone's head. Stone blocked it as best as he could, Hurting his hand while doing so. That was enough time for Herbert T. to land a punch to Stone's mid-section. The punch knocked the wind from Stone. He was still able to avoid the foot coming at his face. Stone ducked just in time, then brought an uppercut to Herbert T's chin. The blow snapped Herbert T's head back and rattled his teeth.

No Neck regained his footing. Shaking his head clear, he stood. When his eyes finally came into focus all he saw was Allen's fist coming towards his face. It seemed to be in slow motion. The first got bigger and bigger the nearer it got to his face.

The blow was solid and painful. Slob and blood flew from No Neck's mouth. He recovered and bent down charging Allen. He head butted Allen in his stomach causing Allen to fall back into more tables, taking No Neck with him. It was a ground fight. The two men struggled back and forth on the floor for the top position.

Stone and Herbert T. squared off into boxing stances. Stone shot a right cross. Herbert T. blocked it and connected by hitting Stone in the face with a left jab. Stone faked a left then followed through with a right, hitting Herbert T. on his left temple. Herbert T's knees buckled. Stone then threw combinations in quick movements to his face. Herbert T. dropped like a sack of potatoes. He lay knocked out on the floor.

No Neck saw what happened to his boss out the corner of his eye. This enraged him giving him crazy man's strength. He managed to get on top of Allen. He was doing some serious damage to Allen when all of a sudden he just fell over. To Allen's surprise, Carol was standing with a broken beer bottle in her hand. She had busted the bottle over No Neck's head. Allen got to his feet smiling at her. she returned him a weak smile dropping the broken bottle and rushing into his arms . Allen looked down at No Neck. "You should have taken the drinks I offered to buy."

Tomorrow was at Stone's side pulling him away from the downed Herbert T. The owner of the club and three men who seemed to be the club bouncers stood in front of the two couples. The bouncers held short clubs in their hands. The club owner pointed to the damage around him and said in a voice that sounded like it had gravel in it. "Who's going to pay for this shit?" he asked.

Stone pulled out a roll of hundreds and threw them to the man, who caught the money in one quick motion. Holding Tomorrow's hand, Stone headed for the door. Allen and Carol brought up the rear. The bouncer and the owner parted allowing them to leave. Just as they reached the door, the owner looked at the two men that were out cold on his floor and said, "I know Herbert T. and I know he more than likely started this mess. But a word of warning, watch your backs. He won't take to getting his ass beat in front of all these people."

"Yeah, he moved on me and mines first. Give him this message. This is over and forgotten, but if he brings any trouble to me or my loved ones, I will visit it back on him one hundred fold, without compunction," warned Stone.

The four were back on the high way heading back home on 1-94 West. They spoke to each other about the incident at length. "I apologize for that mishap back there," said Stone.

"No need for you to apologize for someone else's stupidity," said Carol.

"Yeah baby, you and Allen were defending our honor. I think that's so sweet," said Tomorrow while planting a kiss on his cheek.

"And you gave him every way out. I even offered to buy them both drinks. Don't beat yourself up for something that was beyond your control," explained Allen.

"Baby, that word you used, 'compunction', what does that mean?" asked Tomorrow.

"When I said I'll have no compunction that means no sense of remorse or guilt,"
answered Stone.

Somehow she knew in her heart that Stone meant it.

"By the way, thank you honey. You're pretty handy with a bottle," said Allen

"Oh baby you're welcome. If I had my gun, I would have shot them both," added Carol.

"I wanted to help my baby but was a bit scared and everything was happening so fast," Tomorrow said.

"Bee Spit, don't you ever get between two men when they are fighting," Stone said with a serious look on his face.

Everyone seriously gave thought to that, then Stone made light of it by saying, "Unless I'm on the bottom. Then you can bust him upside his head with whatever."

They all laughed.

After dropping the girls off, Allen took Stone to his car and parked his. They left in Stone's car and went by their club, Establishment. They spoke to Dwayne about business and their run in with Herbert T. in Detroit. Dwayne wasn't familiar with the name, but he knew the type. He told Allen and Stone that he viewed men like Herbert T. as a waste of skin and wished he'd been there to snap the punk in two like a dry twig. All of them lifted their drinks and toasted to that.

CHAPTER 7

Spook rented two adjoining motel rooms. One they could get high in and the other he called his pleasure room. After everyone cleaned up they all got high a little bit and Crack Pipe began to look for things on the floor. Spook looked at him with contempt.

"What the hell is wrong with you?" asked Spook.

"He can't talk when he gets a good hit like that. He's tweaking," said Isis. Things had changed from when Spook used to free base. Now people used cocaine in the form of crack.

"Tweaking?"

"Yeah, the hit got him real high. Now he's looking for dope in the carpet. People have different tweaks. Some are positive tweaks and other are what you see here, a negative tweak," explained Isis.

"Man, sit yo tweaking ass down somewhere. We got plenty mo dope. You fuckin' with my addiction," shouted Spook.

"It don't matter how much dope you sit in front of him. This is how he enjoys his high."

"This mothafucka might be enjoying his, but he's fucking up mine," said Spook.

Crack Pipe got up from the floor and sat on the bed. He began pulling at the tiny lint balls that were on the blanket. Isis put a rock on her pipe, lit it, and sucked on it hard. Spook watched her chest inflate as she inhaled the smoke.

69

He saw her nipples get hard. The way her lips were on the pipe made him become erect.

"Crack Pipe, me and your sister are going in the other room. I'll leave you some stuff right here on the table. Don't take your tweaking ass outside of this room. We have everything that we need for now. I'm gonna take a couple of these 40 ounces and leave you one. Drink some of this beer to take the edge off. Remember don't go anywhere." Spook led Isis towards the other room. He turned and asked Crack Pipe, "You gonna be alright?"

Crack Pipe looked up at him and nodded his head yes. With one finger he pointed up, pumping his arm up down. Spook wasn't use to this sort of behavior. Lucky for him, he was Isis' brother, because he felt like shooting this mutha fucka. What the fuck was he trying to say?

As if reading Spook's, mind Isis translated, "He's trying to tell you that he's high."

Crack Pipe was glad she translated. He gave them both the thumbs up sign and a half smile showing his missing teeth.

Once they were in the room by themselves, Isis and Spook undressed and went straight to the bed. Spook was like an octopus, all hands.

"Hold on just a sec lover, you lie on your back and let me do you," requested Isis.

Spook lay flat out on the bed, she went into little bag that she kept her paraphernalia in and brought out her glass pipe, lighter, and crack. Isis got down on her knees right between his open legs and took him in her mouth. "Wow he's huge!" she thought to herself. Spook let out a moan. She stopped, put some dope on her pipe, and lit it taking in the smoke. Then she sat her pipe to the side on her jeans and put him back in her mouth, exhaling the smoke on his penis making slurping sounds.

"Damn, yeah bitch; you know what you're doing!" Spook said grabbing her head, pushing and pulling himself in out of her mouth.

She aimed what she could around her neck. She looked up at him and said, "This will be my pearly necklace."

Spook laid there breathing hard, not believing how freaky this bitch was and how this crack hoe made him feel while sucking away his life fluids. She went to the restroom and came out with a damp towel, wiping off her face and neck. Then she put another rock on her pipe. Before she could hit the rock, Spook told her to come back to bed and lay on her back. She laid on her back with her legs wide open. Spook climbed above her, looking down at her pussy while she took another puff off the rock. Spook noticed that her clit was swollen. Hopefully due to her being horny, but it looked as if she been hit between the legs with an ax. Spook guided himself into Isis slowly. She was holding in the smoke that she had just inhaled. She laid her hot pipe down on the bed side table. She started to shake. She wrapped her arms and legs around him, blowing smoke and cumming at the same time.

"Yeah!" said Spook, boosting his ego because he hadn't put it all the way in her yet.

"Oh, oh yeah! Get that pussy baby! This is my tweak. I love having orgasms," cried Isis. Spook gave her every inch, each stroke with great force. She screamed, "Fu, fu, fuck that pussy. Fuck that pussy. You big dick mutha fucka you!" Her head went from side to side. It was like she had become demon possessed.

She had never been fucked like this. It felt like the lining was being torn out of her pussy, but good at the same time. She thought he would split her in two. Right now she didn't care. She loved it rough and painful when she came.

"Take this dick bitch. Take all of it. Do you hear me, huh? Do you hear me you good pussy bitch?" hollered Spook.

"Yes….Yes…Daddy I hear you!"

Spook busted a massive load inside of her. Isis felt the warmth of his nut as he continually stabbed at her pussy. She let go of everything that she believed in, something had snapped in her mind. She was in lust and love with this man who was dicking her down.

She arched her back, screaming, trying her best to become one with his organ that was deep inside of her. "Now that's the way you fuck pussy. I'm cumming all over your dick." Isis looked into his eyes. The love bug had bitten her. It was if another world had opened up to her. Spook had taken her to a place that no other had. Now she was sprung on his dick. In her twisted way of thinking, he was the best thing that happened to her, next to crack, of course.

***

It had been a challenging day. Both Allen and Stone wanted nothing more than some food, shower, and a bed. As they headed out the club, Delsena was on her way in.

"Hi Allen," she said.

Allen said, "Hello Del."

She grabbed Stone's arm, "And how are you doing, good looking?"

"Hey baby, I was just leaving," answered Stone.

"Is Tomorrow taking up all of your time? Or can I get you to dust the cobwebs off my monkey tonight?" Delsena whispered in his ear.

Stone thought to himself that Tomorrow had been taking up all of his time, but he liked it. He loved being with her. She made him feel whole. He knew Tomorrow loved him. She had even began to tell him she loved him more often lately. He had cut off all other females, all but Del. She had been there when he was still struggling.

Part of his financial success was credited to her and her long money that really got him started. She also loved him, so he felt he owed her a debt of gratitude. Plus she also made him feel whole and he loved her too. Stone was coming to the realization that he was caught up in a triangle. He loved them both, but for different reasons. His heart just couldn't make sense of it. However, there was something about Tomorrow that tipped the scales, just a little.

"Come on with me. I have to drop Allen off and then we can see what I can do about that dust on your monkey," said Stone with a smile.

"Honey, I drove my own car, why don't you come with me and let Allen drive your car?" asked Delsena.

"Del, Allen's tired. He drove to Detroit and back earlier. It's been a long day baby."

"Okay, I'll pick you up at your place. I hope you're fully charged, because you'll need every ounce of your strength." She turned on her high heels and walked towards her car. Stone and Allen watched as Delsena switched her perfectly sculptured ass. Every step was like poetry in motion.

"Good night, this morning!" said Allen hypnotized by the sway of her ass. "I can see why you still hanging on to that."

"Yeah, I must admit, she's got Kryptonite between those legs, and a booty that is shockingly remarkable. But like I've been telling you, I'm really thinking about settling down with Tomorrow, and who knows, maybe marriage," said Stone.

"Well, whatever you decide, I'm with you all the way mellow."

"I'm still undecided; right now I'm just trying to line my ducks up in a row."

Just then his mother's word came to mind - It's not always a duck, sometimes it's a duck hunter.

He dropped Allen off and then followed Delsena to her place. Once inside the two had a small drink and Del went to fix their bath water. He made some phone calls. Delsena came back and led him her big, spacious bathroom. That was another plus she had in common with Tomorrow; they were self made women, self contained, not gold diggers. Delsena owned a chain of restaurants left to her by her father who passed away. Her mother was still alive and living somewhere out of state. Delsena made sure she didn't want for anything.

The room was lit with tall candles. The giant tub was filled with milk and rose petals were sprinkled on top of the milk. The bath room was fragrant with Jasmine flowers sitting in a vase near the his and her sink. The setting couldn't have been any nicer. The sounds of Barry White played in the background.

"Del you weren't gone that long, how'd you get all of that milk in the tub so fast?" asked Stone.

"I used a couple boxes of powdered milk. Now let's see about getting you out of those clothes." She stepped to him with nothing underneath her robe. She unzipped his pants, looking up into his eyes.

Stone simply pulled the string on her robe and parted it with both hands. She was a beautiful chocolate woman. Her skin so soft and her body was perfect. She just didn't seem real. Without hesitation, he began kissing her and grabbed a handful of ass. He'd had a long day and from the looks of things, it would even be a longer night. She allowed her robe to drop to the floor, exposing her irresistible body that promised pleasure. He felt himself harden.

***

Allen looked at Carol as she got into her bed,."I'm glad you suggested I come over to your place tonight, it's been a tough day," he said.

"Yeah, Tomorrow is knocked out. She'll probably wake up late. I guess Stone canceled at the last minute. She was hoping he would come with you," said Carol.

"Let's just say he was unavoidably detained and leave it that, Okay?" said Allen as he climbed in bed beside her.

"I'm sure they'll work it out."

Allen began licking her nipples. When he felt them getting hard, he began sucking them.

"Allen you know I can't think when you do that."

She opened her legs hoping he would visit her place with that gifted tongue of his.

"Carol at this point there is very little need for thought process, just relax and allow your body to respond to mine."

He then went back to work on her breast. He slid his hand down to her moist vagina working his fingers back and forth on her clit. This made her hot. She reached and noticed he wasn't hard yet. Her body was responding to his but his wasn't responding to hers. She pushed him onto his back. She climbed on top in the sixty-nine position, offering his face to her pussy as her mouth attacked his dick. She engulfed the head in her mouth and flicked at with it her tongue.

He became erect. "Damn Carol, now you done it. Choke that dick until it pukes," Allen said pulling her ass down to him so her pussy was positioned within his tongue's reach.

Carol was working on his manhood making him feel so good. "Just like that, just like that," he whispered.

He darted his tongue in and out of her vagina, tasting the nectar. At the same time he rubbed her clit with his fingers really fast and with urgency.

"Allen, It's yours. Damn it's yours baby."

They were at it for a while longer when Carol's breathing became much louder. "Baby I'm there. Cum with meeeeee!" breathed Carol as she bared down on him, pressing hard against his rough tongue. Her vaginal secretions flowed.

Allen wasn't far behind. He busted as she played with his sack and licked the head hard. He came with intense pleasure, ejaculating his white fluid. She took it all while still cumming with him, and on him.

"Whoa, that was intense," said Allen, breathing hard.

His body was still feeling the effects when she turned around and straddled him. She inserted him inside her before he went soft. "You make a woman addicted to this dick."

"You make a man overdose on this pussy."

Carol's hips gyrated as she placed both hands on his chest, moaning, moving up and down, enjoying the ride. Sweat glistened from her breasts in the dimly lit room. Allen couldn't help but to watch as she arched her back, he could see himself being swallowed up by the lips on her vagina. It really turned him on to watch it swallow him up with each of her down strokes. "Take me baby. It's yours. I'm all yours."

He grabbed her hips and began to thrust upward, meeting her down strokes. It was like a rodeo show. She was riding and he was bucking hard and wild.
"Ooo-Wee, Allen baby, I'm there, and I'm there, aaaaahhhh, oooh, OOOOh, aaahhh."

He couldn't stand it any longer. Feeling her hot juices on him, he came with all the forces he had. It was like time had stopped. Their bodies were setting off the 4th July fireworks. She lay there on top of him as they both took in deep breaths of air. She rolled over on her back. They laid there covered with sweat, looking up at the ceiling. Before they knew it, both were fast asleep in each other's arms.

CHAPTER 8

"Hello!" said Allen.

"Wake up man. It's a nice sunny day outside," said Spook.

"What time is it?" asked Allen.

"It's 10:30. Where are you?"

"I'm at Carol's. Where you at Spook?"

"I'm at our place, or should I say your place."

"You damn well know what's mine is yours. You gonna be there for a minute?"

"Yeah I'll be here. Don't take too long. I have things to take care of."

"Alright, give me a few. I'll be right there," said Allen.

Allen took a quick shower with Carol. He told her he was going to meet his brother. On his way out he spoke to Tomorrow. She was in the kitchen preparing breakfast. Allen could see and smell grits, eggs, bacon, and French toast. "Morning Tomorrow."

"Oh, hi Allen. You want some breakfast before you go? I've made plenty," she replied.

"It smells good, but I'm in a hurry so I must decline the offer."

Carol entered the kitchen drying her long hair. "Girl you got it smelling good up in here," she said. She kissed Allen on the cheek and he patted her on her ass as he was going out the door.

Carol and Tomorrow were eating breakfast when Tomorrow said, "You and Allen look so good together."

Carol replied with excitement, "Girl, I'm falling in love with that man. He was an animal in bed last night. He sucked this pussy so good I thought the top of my head would cave in. He really took me there."

"I thought I heard some sho-nuff screwing jumping off in your room last night. Stone called. He's going to drop by this afternoon. I love Stone. I just wish he would make up his mind because I can't put up with his other women for too much longer."

"I'd love to see you make it. Everyone knows you make a good couple."

"Don't get me wrong, I knew Stone had other women going into this relationship. But things are different, lately he's been talking about settling down and having children. I told him I won't stop taking the pill until I'm the only one," said Tomorrow.

"Keep this between you, me, and the deep blue sea. Allen was telling me this morning how Stone is thinking of asking you the big question," Carol said as she stabbed another piece of French toast with her fork and put it in her mouth. She knew this would cheer Tomorrow up.

Tomorrow stopped chewing on the bacon she had in her hand. "What big question?" asked Tomorrow, leaning towards Carol making sure she heard her right.

"You know marriage."

Tomorrow smiled from ear to ear. Then the smile disappeared as quick as it had came.

"Tomorrow, why did that smile turn upside down into a frown?" asked Carol.

"I was just thinking. Stone says he's just only seeing Delsena from time to time, and I believe him. So now I'm just wondering if Stone and I got married would that stop our number one paying customer, which we both know is Delsena. She comes every other day and tips extremely well. Would that stop her from coming to the shop?"

The girls looked at each other and busted out laughing. "That's my girl, money always on her mind," said Carol reaching for more French toast.

***

"Hello, Allen speaking."

"Yeah what's crack-ah-lacking?" asked Spook.

"I'm just turning the corner now, I can see the house. Is this van what you're riding in?" asked Allen.

"Yeah, it's mine. I parked the car for a minute. You like it?"

"Spook, I'm sure it suits your purpose."

Allen disconnected their phone conversation and parked in front of his house. The van was parked in the drive way. It was a nice and clean with tinted windows, nice rims, and it was a hoe house on wheels. This was Spooks style. It also had a sun roof, with a hatch that opened to let in fresh air. Smoke was coming from it like a broken chimney.

As Allen walked past the van, he saw a man behind the wheel. The window was open. He just looked straight ahead, like a robot. Was he high? Was that crack he smelled in the air?

Isis was in the rear of the van getting high. Crack Pipe was instructed by Spook not to get high until he was finished driving. Spook didn't like Crack Pipe's tweak. After he hit that shit, he was no good to anyone. Plus his tweak stuck with him for awhile. Spook had never seen anyone's tweak to have such a long hang time.

The two brothers greeted and hugged when Allen entered the house. Allen said, "You look well Spook."

Spook replied, "Yeah well, you know me. I'm doing my own thang. Allen you're looking a bit drained. Carol been sucking you dry?"

Allen ignored the question. "Who is that guy in the van?"

"Oh he's just someone who works for me."

"I smelled crack. Does your boy out in the van use that shit? More importantly, do you use that shit?"

"What I do is my business. I just came by to get my bank and some clothes."

"Spook, I worry about you man. I thought you were going into business with me and Stone."

"Change of Plans lil bro. I made me some big bank doing my own thang. You and Stone keep doing what you do. Besides, I don't like that proper talking nigga no way."

"You're entitled to like who you want but I still worry about you man. I been around dope houses into know crack when I smell that shit Spook. Stone used to be out there on that shit bad. He'll tell you that crack will take you. I don't care how strong you are. I'd appreciate it if you or your friends don't do that stuff here where I lay my head. You're older than me. You know the rules. You don't shit where you lay your head," explained Allen.

"Lil bro, I got me a place of my own and a woman to keep my bed warm. You don't have to worry about me coming around here again, except to visit you from time to time."

"Speaking of woman, have you contacted 5-0?"

"Naw, not yet. I don't have time for their shit. They trying to pin that bullshit on me. Maybe that bitch had it coming," said Spook.

"Spook, no one deserves what Lisa went through. Did you know she has a seventeen year old son? Can you imagine what this must be like for him?" Allen scanned Spook's face to see if he displayed any emotions.

"Spare me the hysterics. I didn't beat or rape her, but it will make the seventeen year old stronger to deal with this world. As for that bitch Lisa, she can suck my dick backwards," sneered Spook, with a very sinister look.

This was not the brother Allen grew up with; this appeared to be a calloused man in self destruct mode. "Spook, she is good people and she works for me. She's part of me and Stone's work force family."

"Look man, the stank hoe ain't dead, right?"

"No Spook, she not dead, but she's hanging on to her life by a thread." Allen walked over to the couch and flopped down. He sat there with his head cradled in both hands. He couldn't stand to even look at his brother at the moment. He couldn't believe what his ears were hearing and found it hard to process.

Allen could remember back when he was young and guys would bully him at school. When Spook found out that this little brother was being bullied, he hunted the bullies down and beat them down. He made sure that the word around on the east side of Detroit was that his brother was not to be messed with, in any shape, form, or fashion. It was the two of them against the world. Coming up in foster homes never really gave them any true any parents to get rooted to, but the two of them were always there for each other. Only now, it was as if his brother was an alien.

Spook looked down at his brother and then went and took a seat opposite him. Without looking at Spook, Allen said, "We care for Lisa. You didn't have to hurt her man."

"Man fuck these lame ass nigga's. They soft as surgical cotton. They need to know Spook is here to get his. I'm from that way."

"Spook, the way you survive in this shit is to be invisible below the radar. Not flamboyant and playing Billy bad ass." Allen looked through his blood stained eyes at this man who sat across from him that he hardly knew anymore.

Spook snapped. "Listen here ,punk ass nigga, I was doing this when yo ass was barely discovering you had a dick. I'll be dammed if my brother is going tell me what I can and can't do around this mutha fucka. Yeah, you and yo boy got a lil something going on, but that's yo way. Who in the fuck are you to judge me? I'm old school. I take what's mine just like the gangsters in the old days," barked Spook.

"Well, who's more foolish? The fool or the fool who follows, huh Spook?"

Spook squinted his eyes. "You better be glad you're my brother or I would break your jaw. I'd fuck yo righteous ass up. You still might get fucked up. You keep talking to me like that," he warned.

"Spook, I think its best you leave," demanded Allen, in a loud voice.

Spook got up and headed for the door, picked up his suit cases then turned and stared Allen in the eyes, "Allen, it's plain to see the police don't have any physical evidence against me or your door would have been kicked in. I'd probably be arrested by now. But just so you know where we stand, fuck that bitch! I want the streets to know that

Detroit is in this bitch. Fuck anyone who steps to me about her and fuck you too! I won't go into hiding from anyone. And a word of advice, I just may fuck your boy Stone up for checking me the other night. So don't get in my way or you'll get rolled over too" warned Spook. He slammed the door as he left.

Allen remembered something that he had read in the bible, John 15:2. "A branch that doesn't bear fruit is cut from the tree." He decided that he must cut Spook off. Allen still had love for his brother, but he couldn't allow Spook to pull him down. The last thing he expected was for trouble to come within the ranks of his family.

Allen asked himself out loud, "What type of monster have I released on this town?"

CHAPTER 9

Sweat gathered at Stone's forehead as he did his last set on the weights. "You ready to call it a day?" asked Stone.

"Yeah," replied Allen. The men showered and left the gym that they frequented for their work outs.

Allen informed Stone about his encounter with Spook. It didn't surprise Stone. Stone told Allen that he would avoid Spook, due to him being his brother. Stone also told him that he'd have to do what he must if cornered.

"I don't understand him Stone. I mean, I tried to have things in order for him, and there is nothing I wouldn't have done for my brother. He was argumentative and confrontational. Stone he had this look in his eyes... the best I can explain it is they seemed void of life. He was a whole other person," explained Allen.

"Allen, Spook knows right from wrong. And knowing you the way I do, I'm sure you tried your best to talk to him. From what you told me, he didn't just want to harm me, he threatened you if you got in his way. Hopefully he was just blowing off steam. However we must assume he's serious."

"Well let's hope he's not. Things were going pretty smooth before he came to town. I'll see you at the club later."

"Alright, I'm going to Tomorrow's house for a few hours. You going to be okay Allen?"

"Yeah, I'm trying to wrap my head around all that's been going on. You know me. I'll bounce back."

Allen got out the car and went into his home. Stone saw his friend was troubled. There was very little he could do at this point. He had much love for Allen, prayerfully these brothers would work things out. It's a hurting thing when you're at odds and ends with a loved one and they just won't seem to listen to reason. Allen had been doing well for himself and now this thing happened with his brother. Stone would hate to see Spook bring out Allen's bad side. After all, they were of the same blood.

***

Water ran like small rivers from the contours of her caramel body. She adjusted the shower head to one her favorite settings. The mild pulse of a jet stream bounced off her breast. The hot water felt good on her skin. She heard the chime of the cell phone on the sink. Tomorrow turned the water off and wrapped a big towel around her body and stepped out for the phone. She looked at the caller ID. It was Stone.

"Hi baby, where you at?" she answered.

"I'm outside your bathroom door. May I come in?" asked Stone.

"Yes silly, you don't have to ask. Why are you, calling? You could've just came in."

"Well I figured everyone deserves a certain degree of privacy. Besides that, I love hearing your voice."

"Are you going to stand outside that door or come on here where I can lay my hands on you?" asked Tomorrow.

"You know, that sounds real tempting. Permission to come aboard Miss Lady?"

"Permission granted Mr. Man."

When Stone opened the door he was naked with just his cell phone to his ear. He had been undressing the whole time. Stone came in and closed the door. Tomorrow's eyes bucked wide, this was the last thing she expected to see. It was good Carol had left.

"Baby why are you standing at my bath room door buck booty naked?" asked Tomorrow.

He went over and removed her towel, letting it fall to the floor.

"Because I wanted us to have matching outfits," answered Stone. He pulled her into his arms.

 She said, "But we're not wearing any outfits," looking up at him.

"My point exactly, birthday suits are all that's required."

He began kissing her slow and passionately. He started to grow. She felt his hardness on her skin and became moist between her legs. Stone guided her back to the shower and turned the water on. Then backed her against the shower wall.

Her nipples were in his mouth as the water from the shower beat a low rhythm on their bodies. He ran his tongue up and down her neck slowly. Tomorrow began to moan and put one of her legs on the rim of the tub, allowing him easy access. She guided him inside her. The leg that was on the rim of the tub was now over the bent part of his arm as he held it there and drove his member all the way to the hilt, slamming in and out of her. She bit at his shoulder lightly as she absorbed each of his welcomed thrusts. Tomorrow was taking in big gulps of air, crying, and sinking her nails onto his back.

"Oh Stone. Yes that's my spot baby…..Oh …Oh … yes. Keep hitting it right there," she cried.

She held on to him as if her life depended on it. Their bodies slammed together as the water continued its beat. Stone became overwhelmed with each thrust that brought him closer and closer to his peak. "Tomorrow it's so good baby, what are you doing to me?" he said.

He knew what was coming next. So he braced his free hand on the shower wall and plunged himself into the depths of her vagina, depositing his seed. She was closer to her climax now and felt every bit of his shaft and cum planted deep inside of her. She let go making moaning sounds as vaginal secretions mixed with his sperm.

They finished showering and then proceeded to her bed. The room was very feminine with the purple lace bed coverings. Stone coaxed her onto her back and began to lick and suck at her hardened nipples. She pulled his head up and kissed him. "I love you so much Stone," she said looking deep into his eyes.

"I love you too baby. More then you will ever know." He finally said the words.

His tongue moved tongue down her neck back past her breast, pressing hard making a circular motion in her naval. She began to lick her lips and spread her legs wide apart anticipating the next spot he would visit. Then he parted her pubic hairs, vaginal lips, and blew his breath softly on her clit. Tomorrow looked down at this man she loved with an intense gaze as her clit began to swell.

He said, "Will you marry me?"

She was flabbergasted. "Stone, I … I ….I can't believe you asked me that while down there in my bush! Hell yes, you know I will. I love you Stone," she said with much happiness in her voice.

"I love you, I wanted you to always remember this moment," Stone said while looking into her eyes. Then he licked her pussy.

Her senses were on fire from his touch. She sucked in air through her clenched teeth.

"Consider this an ambush," he said and licked her furiously.

She moaned softly, smiling to herself. Feeling her climax coming she rubbed her nipples with one hand and grabbed his hair with the other, pulling his head farther into her pussy.

"Stay ….right …..there," she said in between breaths.

Tomorrow was overcome with stimulation. She held his head right at that very spot and came. Sighs of pleasure escaped her lips and juices flowed. Moments later, she lay there breathing hard, allowing the intense feeling to subside then sat up and took her dry towel and wiped his face. They kissed feverishly. Without saying a word she got on all fours. She placed two pillows under her head and laid her head sideways so she could look back at him.

She hiked her butt up in the air for him to hit it from the rear. Stone positioned himself on his knees behind her, putting one hand on her ass as he guided himself into her wet waiting pussy, doggie style.

"Damn baby you make me just want to get off by your touch alone," she said still looking back at him.

"Give it to me baby, your husband to be."

With every push his own pleasure seemed to amplify. He couldn't help but to let out a low grown. Tomorrow was meeting each push with her own sighs of pleasure, matched by his and coupled with heavy breathing. As he thrust into her, he reached around with his finger and started tapping lightly on her clit.

"Oh Stone, that's right …..that's right …..there…. there baby. Make me cum!"

She shuddered and hummed the whole time she climaxed. Then she collapsed onto her stomach, with Stone still on top. Stone caught his breath and then turned her over on her back and he rolled over on top of her. While still semi-hard he rubbed it gently on her clit.

"Oh my goodness…..Yes……Yes…Oh baby," Tomorrow cooed while wrapping her legs around him plunging him inside her well lubricated vagina.

Stone grunted and moaned as sweat beaded over their bodies. Tomorrow braced herself against the headboard. She bit her bottom lip and threw everything she had at him. Stone did his best to beat up the pussy. He wanted to feel her cum again but he can't wait any longer because she was throwing pure pussy at him.

"Baby takes all of this," Stone breathed.

She squealed and her body quivered. Feeling his hot sperm makes her cum, she screamed out loud in ecstasy. They both lay there fully spent, taking in lungs full of air. Stone begins to roll over on her feeling fully drained. Then she stops him from pulling out. She liked the feeling of him inside her and the beat of their hearts, beating as one. "Stay right there baby, let me go to sleep with you inside me." To her surprise, Stone was asleep before she completed her sentence.

CHAPTER 10

"Aaah shit!" yelled Crack Pipe as he dropped the tire gauge that he used to smoke his crack. He couldn't keep a glass pipe. He always got them too hot and they broke. The tire gauge would get hot but would not break. He called it his trusty straight shooter. Crack Pipe had just taken a small hit of rock but he got it too hot, so he dropped it on the vans carpeted floor. Spook and Isis were in the back of the van getting high.

"Mutha fucka, what are you trying to do? Burn this mutha fucka down?" Spook said with anger as crack smoke flowed from his mouth.

They were in the parking lot across the street from one of Stone and Allen's after hour gambling joints. Spook had told Crack Pipe that while they were on their mission he could smoke, but only a little at a time because he didn't want him stuck on stupid.

Crack Pipe protested as he picked up the tire gauge with a napkin. "Well if you give me enough dope to get high, I wouldn't be burning my straight shooter up," he complained while he picked off the burnt pieces of carpet that were stuck to his tire gauge.

"That's the point. I don't need you stuck. Wait until we get back to the hotel room. Isis smokes this stuff and she can still function. This shit affects people differently. Take you for instance, you tweak all over the place. Here, I'm going to give you one mo hit and then you chill until we finish here alright?"

Just knowing that he had another hit coming for now renewed his happiness. "Okay. Okay. I'll chill till we get to the room after this one," said Crack Pipe.

Spook tossed Crack Pipe a rock from the small pile on the vans table. Crack Pipe tried catching it. The rock bounced from his hand. He tried recovering it with his other hand and fumbled, causing it to fall on the floor of the van. He knew it was somewhere in this carpet. Spook realized his mistake in throwing Crack Pipe the rock, because he was on all fours looking for the rock. Now his tweak was really on.

Spook's plan was to become rich and powerful. He'd start by taking over small business by offering some types of protection. Gangsters had been doing it for years. But for now he'd have to concentrate his efforts on small businesses that also had illegal activities on the side, like robbing dope houses. This would better his chances of the police not being called. Not knowing much about this town, Spook relied on Isis and Crack Pipe to provide him with location of other drug dens. Spook and Isis stepped from the van. It was a mildly cold night with a full moon, which gave the surroundings a light hue. Spook remembered reading somewhere that the full moon was also known as the hunter's moon. Well tonight he was on the hunt. He and Isis sported long maxi black coats.

Isis wore a black sports bra under her coat. She had a Glock 9mm semi- automatic attached to a shoulder rig, one of the guns they had taken from the dope dealers. Spook wore black cargo pants with a black wife beater tank top underneath his coat. The .45 desert Eagle hung from his shoulder rig. Wearing all black was Isis's idea. Spook was really into this small woman who seemed to be down with her man. This mulatto woman had light features and plenty of heart, but her crack addiction was serious. She went through the stuff as if it was candy.

Once they became more established, maybe just maybe he could get her off the stuff. He couldn't really say much because he also used. Spook picked this drug house because Isis told him they hadn't been selling for that long and they didn't care who they sold to as long as they got money. Crack Pipe was left to look after the van. Spook left him another rock and told him not to go anywhere and to stay out of sight. Spook and Isis walked to the back door of the drug house. Isis knocked on the door. Someone peeped through the peep hole and then opened the door.

"Yeah, how much?" was all the door man asked. His breath smelled like someone had shit in his mouth.

"I'm spending $200.00 and I want to smoke it here with my man," said Isis. She gestured towards Spook.

"Damn girl! You ain't never spent that much money at one time. You must have hit the lottery or something, huh Isis?"

"Naw, I wish. My new man here keeps me rolling in the stuff," replied Isis. She grabbed Spook's massive arm.

"Well you know It's another $10 per person that smokes here, so with two that adds up to $20 smoking fee."

Isis didn't remember a smoking fee the last time she had gotten high here. In fact Smooth and Slick encouraged smokers to smoke here in case someone was a cop. Plus, anyone who got high and had money would more than likely spend more money since the drugs was readily available. Isis figured the doorman thought he could get his little hustle on this way.

"Jay when did anyone have to pay to smoke here?" said Isis showing her anger with both of her hands on her hips.

Spook spoke before Jay the doorman could reply, "Money's no problem. Can we come in or must we stand out here for everyone to see?"

Jay looked at this dark man and waved them both inside. "Give me the $200.00 and I'll be back with your stuff."

Jay had a medium build. He still had some weight on his bones for a smoker, but his teeth had seen better days and he smelled of sweat with the funk of an unwashed body.

"Oh hell naw, nigga! You know I don't go through yo ass for shit. Here take yo $20 for us to smoke here, but you know I can buy from Smooth and Slick my damn self. You ain't gone bring my shit back short. I know that you smoke and you pinch off other peoples shit. Now go get them or we'll take that $20.00 back and move on to the next spot." Isis said with fire in her voice.

Jay wanted to slap this crack hoe down, but he decided against it when he saw the sinister look on Spook's face. He accepted the terms and told them to wait in the basement with the others. There was an open door that led

97

to the kitchen and another that led to the basement. They went down the dimly lit wooden steps. Once they reached the bottom, Spook felt how cold it was. No heat was good. They could keep their coats on without being suspicious. A white male and white female were sitting on an old couch getting high at the other end of the basement. They also wore their coats. Both looked up at Spook and Isis with their big saucer like eyes.

The female smiled, "Isis, what's up girl?"

"Hey Michelle," answered Isis. The women ran to each other and embraced. "Come here. Let me introduce you to my new man," said Isis.

"Spook kept his eyes on the man on the couch. He was sweating and his hair was all over his head. He was oblivious to what going on around him. His mouth kept moving from side to side. This was common with most smokers. It was known as marble mouth. Then Spook's attention went back to the white girl.

"Baby, this is Michelle, she use to be my wifey. We still get down like that sometimes and you can join if you like. Can we take her with us?" asked Isis as if she was asking to bring home a pet.

"Isis, stay focused on our mission," Spook reminded her.

Then Michelle added, "Isis you see I got a sucker on the hook."

Michelle nodded to marble mouth sitting on the couch. He put what little dope he had left on his pipe. Michelle and

98

Isis were of the same cloth they knew the streets, and hustled them. Spook took a long look at the woman, not bad at all he thought to himself. She had long, blond hair with blue eyes and a nice shape. She was a bit taller than Isis. She also had nice round breast. She was in her mid-twenties with a ghetto booty supported by her child bearing hips. He couldn't help but to notice this white woman had a sexy over bite. Spook peeped that moment she spoke. She would surely please any man that bedded her. Plus, she looked and smelled clean. Information is power. Maybe he could use her for information among other things. Spook knew he needed women who were seasoned with street smarts.

Spook said, "Don't worry Michelle, I'll give you all the dope you can smoke. Just do as I say. If you don't have a problem with that, we'll get along fine."

Michelle looked at Isis. Isis knew her thoughts and nodded her head with a smile. They went over to the couch where the man sat. Spook broke out some dope of his own, giving everyone a rock. The older man on the couch looked at them, took the rock and nodded a motion of thanks and continued back in his zone.

Michelle looked at the old man with distaste. "Isis, he's about broke, and stuck on stupid. I'm with you guys," Michelle said, liking how things were shaping up.

They heard footsteps coming down the stairs. Spook looked at Michelle and said quickly, "Get rid of old boy. Tell him you're ready to go and to meet you in his car."

Michelle started thinking that Spook had changed his mind about taking her with him and Isis, so she voiced her thoughts by saying, "I said I was going with you guys."

"Just do as I say now!" Spook demanded in a low but deep voice.

Michelle whispered in the man's ear, "I'm horny. Meet me in your car. I'm ready to fuck."

The man smiled and stood. He put his belongings in his pockets and gave Michelle's breast a squeeze. He headed for the steps passing Smooth and Slick.

"You straight old man or do you need some mo?" asked one of the dope dealers.

"I'm okay for now," said the old man as he continued his walk up the stairs.

One of the dope dealers cupped both of his hands on his mouth and yelled up the steps to the doorman, "Let this tweaking son of a bitch out."

As they came to the bottom of the steps they noticed a real dark nigga they had never seen before. "Hey Isis, who that nigga you got with you?" asked Smooth.

Smooth and Slick stood at the bottom of the stairs with their hands on the guns that they openly displayed in their waist band of their pants. Spook tried his best to play the part of a fiend that was really high.

"This is my man, Spook. Spook this is Slick and that's Smooth," said Isis pointing to each man.

100

Both men kept their eyes on Spook. "You ain't 5-0 are you?" asked Slick.

As if on cue, Spook took a long hit, taking in lungs full of smoke, and smoke was coming from his mouth when he said, "Naw, I'm far from the po-po, man."

"So how much you want?" asked Smooth. He was getting impatient.

"$200 worth, so can I party with these ladies."

"Show us some cheese," requested Smooth.

Spook stood and slowly reached into his pockets. He brought out a wad of money and tore off $200. Everyone saw the big wad of money. Spook noticed the greed in the eyes of Slick and Smooth. He handed the money to Isis, who stood and walked over to the where Slick and Smooth stood, handing them the money.

Slick took the money and then giving Smooth the okay nod. Smooth handed Isis the dope saying, "Where yo silly ass brother at?"

"I haven t seen him in days," replied Isis.

"When you see him tell him we got some work for him. You're looking good. Look at you all cleaned up. You can leave them down here and come have some fun with me and Slick. I remember you can suck a mean dick," said Slick while gripping his genitals through his pants.

Spook wanted to explode. Isis was his girl now and he wouldn't stand for any man to disrespect him. He had to play cool for now because when the time was right he would lay down his jack move.

"May be some other time, I just told y'all I'm with my man. Let us enjoy our high for a while and I'll see what he has to say."

"Michelle, is your boy coming back? Or are you spending some more money? If not you got to bounce," said Smooth.

"He went to get some more money," said Michelle. She was a bit nervous and did not really know what to say. "Anyway I'm hanging with my girl and her man."

"You know the rules buy or bounce," added Smooth.

Spook tore off another $200 and gave it to Michelle. The money and the dope exchanged hands. Then just like Isis, she switched her ghetto booty back to the couch handing Spook the product.

"Keep spending like this we can shut the mutha fucka down early," said Slick.

The door man came down the steps.

"What the hell you want Jay?" asked Slick.

"Can I take a break down here with them for a while?" he asked pointing to the couch where the three were getting high.

"Hell naw! Use that $20.00 he got from us for his little smoking fee. Jay you ain't gonna sit yo begging ass around us fucking up my high," complained Isis.

Spit flew out of Slick's mouth, "Shut the fuck up bitch! You ain't running shit but yo mouth. Jay, give me that $20.00. You know better than to hustle my custos,"

"You suppose to give me some dope for watching the door," said Jay.

"Bitch ass mutha fucka, I'll pay you when I'm ready. Drop the twenty before I take it and kick yo stanking ass, and then throw you out in the snow," demanded Slick. He walked up to Jay.

The doorman unwillingly gave up the money. Smooth tossed a rock on the floor in front of him. "When you're done with that post yo ass back on that door. If you hear someone knocking, get up there," Smooth said.

Slick started back up the stairs then turned and looked at Spook, "Oh, and when y'all want some mo just holla or send Jay up to get us." The two men disappeared up the steps.

Jay started to sit with them on the couch, but the look Spook gave him, he knew better to stay his distance. For now, he'd be content with his crack sitting on the steps. Michelle, Isis, and Spook went over some details in whispered voices due to Jay not being too far out of listening range. Michelle told them that the old man would be gone by now. He wouldn't wait for long in his car in this part of the hood, besides he was in a twenty five year marriage with a controlling wife. He didn't want her or the kids to know that he smoked dope and not to mention him getting some pussy on the side.

It had been all of fifteen minutes and Jay had smoked all he had. He started picking up debris from the steps, hoping there were some pieces of crack he'd dropped. Isis slipped one hand down her spandex pants and began to play with herself while rubbing on Michelle titties with her other hand. Michelle rubbed Spook's manhood through his pants. Jay was moving around too much on the steps and making unnecessary noises. This aggravated Isis. She stopped rubbing Michelle's breast but kept fingering herself.

Then said Isis "Oh hell naw, you gotta get you tweaking ass back up stairs, you fucking up with my addiction" Repeating the words she had heard Spook say.

Spook decided he'd waited long enough. It was time to get Slick and Smooth back down here and do his jack move. Jay ignored the tongue lashing Isis gave him and kept picking things from the floor. He was high and paranoid at the same time. Spook stopped what he was doing and yelled at Jay, "Go get your boys."

Jay never looked up from what he was doing. Michelle went to the bottom of the stairs, cupped her hands to her mouth, and yelled for Slick and Smooth. Slick came down the steps, this time alone.

"Yeah what's up?" He saw Jay doing his thing on the floor. Slick kicked him in his leg and Jay rolled over with a moan. "Get Yo stanking ass back upstairs on the door!" shouted Slick.

The disgruntled doorman limped his way back up the steps.

"Yeah what y'all want? Don't ask for any damn credit," said Slick. He was feeling confident now that he and his boy made a show of force earlier. He was getting ready to make some money off these fiends. Upstairs, he and Smooth figured the two of them needed to go down stairs when Jay had told them that Isis had brought some big black unknown man. So the two went downstairs together as a precaution. Now, Slick and Smooth reasoned all dope fiends were docile when they got high, so Slick and his gun would be enough. How wrong they were.

Spook had only gotten so high. The rest was a show to lure them into a false sense of security. It was all orchestrated into what was about to take place now. "I need about $100 mo," said Spook. He slurred his words and faked marble mouth. Slick smiled, then held out his hand. This time Spook got up and walked over to the man. He handed him a hundred dollar bill. When Slick went to hand Spook the dope, Spook's hand shot up to his neck choking him up against the wall, stopping him from yelling for help. His other hand stopped Slick from reaching for his gun.

Spook cut off Slick's windpipe. The air his brain needed to function was quickly being depleted. His strength was leaving him rapidly. Naturally, he abandoned his attempts to reach for his gun and went into survival mode. He tried desperately to remove Spooks vise grip hand from around his neck. In a sick way, this excited the girls. Spook removed Slick's gun and tossed it over to the girls. Isis handed it to Michelle, who was in shock at the present situation. The gun was a .380 semi-auto. Spook dragged Slick away from the stairs so no one could see from upstairs what going on. Slick was easy to move. Spook moved him around as if he was a rag doll. He positioned Slick face up, took out his desert Eagle, and placed the gun to his left eye. Slick was about to go unconscious when Spook removed his hand from around his neck. He placed it roughly over his mouth. Although Spook's hand was over his mouth, Slick welcomed any air he could get. He took air into his lungs.

Spook said, "Listen very closely. You're going to do exactly what I tell you. If you try to yell or anything that displeases me, the bullet that's in the chamber of this gun will bore a hole through your head. If you understand, nod your head."

Slick nodded his head, cursing himself for letting this dope fiend get the drop on him. This big man had a big gun to his eye, the knee on his chest hurt like hell, and this mutha fucka's breath stunk of crack.

"How many people upstairs?" asked Spook, removing his hand from Slick's mouth.

"Just Smooth, the doorman, and some broad."

"Call the doorman down here first."

"Hey Jay, come here for a sec," yelled Slick.

"Isis get over there," said Spook motioning with his head.

Isis went over by the steps so that she couldn't be seen. Michelle was still in awe by the events that were unfolding so she just sat there with the gun in hand looking wide-eyed. A part of her liked this gangster shit. She was thinking maybe she could loosen up and let out her wild side. Michelle was pretty much raised in the country. She was a tomboy brought up with two older brothers who were field hands growing up as boys. She had been knocked around enough to know how to defend herself well.

Her brothers went on to become doctors with family practices out of state. Michelle had spent most of her adult life in th neighboring town of Kalamazoo. It was 18-20 miles from Battle Creek. From time to time she would visit Battle Creek, to look up Isis and hustle. The lure of the fast life in the streets was far more addictive to her than the drugs.

When Jay got to the bottom of the stairs he saw the dark man with a gun to Slick's face. His mind was processing this when Isis slammed a gun upside his temple. Jay went crashing down to the floor fast and hard. Trickles of blood came from the wound on the side of his head as he lay there, out for the count.

Michelle ran to Isis side. They both hovered over the doorman's unconscious form admiring Isis's handy work. Spook wanted to laugh, but held himself in check. He watched the girls drag Jay over by the couch. Spook instructed the girls to hold their guns on Slick. He positioned himself by the steps. "Now call your boy Smooth down here," demanded Spook.

Michelle stood over Slick with her own gun pointed at Slick's head. She shook nervously while Isis stood over him aiming her gun at his manhood. "You heard what my man said," added Isis.

"You bitches are dead!" Slick said angrily.

Spook said, "Call him now, or I'll have her shoot off your left nut."

Isis pressed her gun to his private parts and cocked the hammer back. The wicked click of the gun gave no room for doubt, she would do it. From the look on her face, she'd enjoy it. Slick did as he was told. There was no answer. He yelled for Smooth again. Still no answer. The third time he called for Smooth and didn't receive an answer, they all realized that from this point on things could get real ugly and problematic. The only way out was up those steps.

"Stay here and keep an eye on these two. If they give you any problems, shoot to kill," was all Spook said.

He started up the steps taking two at a time. At the top landing he noticed that the door straight ahead was the door that led outside. The door on the left that led to the rest of the house was closed. It wasn't that way when he and Isis entered the house. He checked the door to see if it was locked. It wasn't. Was this a trap? Was Smooth waiting on the other side, waiting to blow him away? There was only one way to find out. Spook turned the door knob and pushed the door open, and slowly walked through.

***

Isis and Michelle held their guns on Slick. Occasionally, they looked over at the doorman, making sure he was still knocked out.

"You bitches know there is nowhere you can hide. I will hunt you and that black ass nigga down no matter where you go," warned Slick. He saw that his threats weren't getting him anywhere he tried a different approach. "Let me loose and I'll give both you some dope and I'll forget that you betrayed me."

Michelle was no longer nervous. She held her gun on him, but it was shaking more than ever now. Not out of fear for herself, but more so for Slick, because she wanted to kill so bad she could taste it.

"Shut the fuck up. We still remember how you use to give us crumbs for us to suck your nasty ass dick. We don't owe you shit," said Isis.

"At least you got paid. You crack bitches are all the same. All you want is dope. No sense of direction whatsoever. Now give one of those guns and let me handle my business with that mutha fucka up them steps and I'll give you both a half ounce to smoke."

"Naw, my man got us covered. Damn you, the worm has turned. It ain't no fun when the rabbit got the gun, huh Slick?"

"You sluts are dead," Slick said with rage all over his face.

"Michelle , keep your gun pointed at his head. I'm gonna find something to tie him up with so we can smoke us some dope while we wait."

"I have a better idea. You keep him covered while I take my pantyhose off. You can tie him up with those," mused Michelle.

Michelle took off her pants and removed the pantyhose that she had worn under them. Isis noticed the light shining off Michelle's pubic hair. She put her pants back on. Then Michelle asked, "Do you have any panties on?"

"Yeah I got some on," answered Isis.

"Well take them off. We'll use them for a gag, but hurry because when I had my pants off my pussy got cold."

Isis liked the way Michelle was thinking, and removed her panties, she saw what Michelle meant about the cold. Her bottom was freezing so she hurried putting her pants back on. Michelle watched Isis' bare bottom with equal interest. Then Michelle took a knife from her pocket and cut her pantyhose in two. One half for Slick's feet, the other half for his hands. Slick protested the time with threats. She then took her position back over Slick with the gun pointed at his head so Isis could tie him up.

"If you move, I'll be forced to put one in your melon."

Slick wanted to try these bitches, but not at the expense of his life. Hell he and Smooth were selling this shit for someone else. That someone else would kill him for sure, if they got jacked by some damn dope fiends. Isis had tied his hands and was tying his feet. Michelle stole a glance over at the doorman. Slick saw his chance and kicked at Isis' face. She saw it coming and tried to move out of the way. His foot caught her shoulder knocking her backwards. Michelle wanted to shoot him but thought better of it because she didn't want to alert anyone upstairs. No doubt they all would be killed, plus Spook was up there in stealth mode. She became very angry and brought the butt of her gun down on his forehead causing Slick to cover his face for the next blow, which gave Isis enough time to recover.

He stopped his attempt when he saw they both had fight in them. Isis stood over him breathing hard. She brought the butt of the gun down on his head. It made a gash across his forehead. "Michelle take out your knife and put it to his neck. If he moves, cut him deep." .

Isis got Slick's hands and feet tied. They sat right by him on the floor getting high and blowing smoke at his face. Slick couldn't say anything because Isis's panties were stuffed in his mouth. Michelle looked at Slick for a moment. She took out her knife so that Slick could see the light glimmer from the blade. Isis watched with interest.

"So you want to kick my girl huh?" Michelle said. She removed Slick's shoes and socks. Slick looked on in horror and tried to scream as the gleaming blade sliced into his skin.

CHAPTER 11

Spook found himself in the kitchen. Dishes were piled high in the sink and takeout food containers were everywhere. An expensive coat was laid across one of the chairs. From a glance he noticed a scale, some weed, cigars, probably for rolling blunts, and several 40 ounces on the dining room table. There were two duffel bags in the chairs. Spook took a peak in both of the bags. One held bricks. It was powder cocaine and the other held stacks of money. Jackpot! He moved slowly with the .45 Desert Eagle in front of him. He didn't see or hear anyone. Spook walked down the hallway when he heard the faint sound of music coming from one of the three closed doors or the stair case leading to the second floor.

The house was so big that he hadn't heard the music from the basement. Slick said that the only people up here were Smooth and some broad. He couldn't have been lying so it would be best to check the rooms. The first door he came to was unlocked. He opened the door and made a sweep of the room with it. No one was there. Spook repeated the same process in the next room. No one was in there either. The last door he opened was the rest room. Damn still no one. He'd have to go upstairs.

Spook thought he could just take the duffel bags and be on his way. The thought was dismissed because he wanted any and all the money those pushers possessed. Also, they knew what he looked like. He climbed the stairs slowly.

The house wasn't that bad for a drug den. It wasn't run down and mildly furnished. This house couldn't have been in business for that long. It didn't show any sign of decay or neglect by long drug usage of its occupants. He thought about the drugs and coat downstairs. The drugs may have been a fresh shipment and whoever owned that expensive fur, had money or was connected to money. Spook eased carefully to the top of the stairs. He put his back to the wall. He stood there for a few moments because it was so dark. He allowed his eyes to adjust to the darkness. The music was louder now. It was coming from the room at the end of the hall. He checked the first door. It was locked but no noise was heard from within. He went to last door still moving slowly. The door was slightly ajar. He entered the dimly lit room. What Spook saw froze him in his tracks. Shock and disbelief overcame him.

***

Isis and Michelle were having a good old time. Michelle had loosened up even more after she removed Slick's shoes and socks. She thought back to the time Slick and Smooth had accused her of stealing their dope. No dope had been stolen. It was just their way of getting her to pay up with her body. They were brutal with her and then kicked her out. The only reason she was here tonight was because no one else in this town had any drugs that were any good. She knew that if she hung around from time to time, bought dope, and got high, they would relax and forget. When the time was right it would be payback time.

She had put it all behind her, until now. She took the knife and ran small incisions along the bottom of both his feet. He tried screaming in pain, but Isis' panties quieted his cry. He was sweating like a Hebrew slave. Michelle and Isis took turns putting their hot pipes to his bleeding feet. Slicks body bucked as his seared flesh protested the increase in temperature. His breathing became labored.

Isis removed her panties from his mouth, giggling the whole time. "So how does my pussy taste?"

Slick spat in her face. Isis wiped the spit from her face then stuffed her panties so far in his mouth that he almost choked on them. "Let's give him a golden shower," she suggested.

"Honey you were reading my mind," said Michelle looking like a child opening a Christmas gift.

Both women squatted over Slick's face and took a long piss while smoking on their cigarettes. The golden streams of urine drenched his face. The odor was pungent. All Slick could do was move his head from side to side. He tried to avoid the stench of the loud smelling piss. When they finished Michelle sat on his chest and rubbed her vagina back and forth to dry herself off. Then she passed gas while still on him, just before standing and pulling up her pants.

Isis really liked this. She repeated the same process. They were sure he was cussing them out from the sounds he made. Isis stood and pulled her pants up. She gave her girl some play for defiling that nigga. She bent over towards him. "Now, I'm going take these pissy panties from yo mouth. We don't want you to die just yet, but you better behave yourself. Do you hear me?"

Slick nodded his head. Isis pinched her nose with one hand and with the other pulled the panties from his mouth with two fingers, holding them far from her body. She dropped them beside his head in the piss puddle. Steam came from the warm urine mixed with cold air. Slick coughed, glad to be able to breathe fresh air again, even though it was contaminated with crack smoke. A thought occurred to Isis. She should see how much money he had in his pockets.

"What the hell is wrong with y'all? Y'all done went crazy. Michelle I know Isis' elevator don't go all the way to top, but I'm surprised that you would do something like this," said Slick with a shaky voice. He coughed and looked back and forth at the two women.

Isis said to Michelle, "Run his pockets."

Michelle checked his pockets. Slick continued, "My feet are bleeding bad. I need some medical attention. Y'all gonna let me lay here and bleed to death?"

"You won't bleed to death. We burned you with our pipes to close your wounds. Plus, I got pleasure watching you squirm and scream like a bitch," said Michelle.

Isis laughed at what her girl Michelle had just said, Michelle had found some money, car keys, condoms, and his cell phone. She put everything into her purse.

Slick asked, "So what y'all gonna do with me?"

"Don't know yet, that's up to my man. You just lay there and be quiet he'll be back soon," replied Isis.

Michelle and Isis sat several feet from Slick on floor away from their piss puddle with their get high material in between them. Both of them were taking hits on their pipes and blowing smoke in each other faces when a fist slammed into Isis head, knocking her over sideways. The blow caused her to see lights of all colors. Her pipe flew from her hand, breaking as it hit the floor. Michelle tried to respond to the threat, too late; the same fist was now making its way towards her.

***

Spook just refused to believe the image before him. What his eyes beheld would forever be tattooed on his brain. There were two people on the bed, a man and a woman. Spook recognized the man. It was Smooth and some over sized woman that Spook had never seen. Was this the woman with expensive fur downstairs? This woman had a somewhat cute face, however she was huge. She had folds of fat overlapping fat. They both were naked. Smooth was on his stomach and she was on top with a strap on dick. She pushed it into him hard.

They were so engrossed in their morbid sex act, they didn't notice Spook. It took all his strength to keep from laughing out loud. Their backs were to him and Smooth was in much pain. You could tell by the way he grunted and tensed his body with each thrust that this big woman stabbed him with. She thrusted the strap on penis in him and pulled his head back at the same time.

"You like it when Big Mama give it to you like that, don't you? I said, don't you boy?" she yelled in his ear.

116

"Yeah …..Yeah Big…Big Mama, oooh, you're ripping me," cried Smooth.

"Shut up and take it like a man you big ass baby. I been wanting yo tight ass for a long time, I told you if you kept selling dope for me and my brother, I was gonna get this ass in bed someday. You a fine mutha fucka. I'm gonna pay you like we agreed so shut up. This ass is mine for a whole hour. Now tell big mama that you like it!"

Smooth felt like his guts were being torn out. She let go of his head and pulled him up so that they both were on their knees, doggie style. She smacked his ass. Sweat jumped off her as each massive breast flopped up and down. The big woman grunted like an ape. It seemed as if she was getting off. The room smelled like shit. A part of Spook felt sorry for Smooth. This woman was pile driving a fake dick up his ass and she had no mercy for him. The sight alone began to make Spook sick to his stomach. He stood there with the big gun aimed at them. Never in his entire life had he seen such a twisted display of sex with man and woman. This type of shit in his day was unheard of. Spook was totally discombobulated.

***

The blow glanced off the side of Michelle's temple causing her to bite her tongue. Her slight movement saved her from the full impact. She turned to see Jay, the doorman, bring his foot high in the air to stomp her head.

She kicked out at the leg he was standing on. His leg flew out from under him. He crashed to the floor beside

Michelle. She was fast. Michelle got on top of Jay and used both hands. She punched wildly at his face, connecting with every blow. Jay threw a lucky punch upwards that connected with Michelle's forehead. The punch knocked her off of him. Jay was on his feet now and she was still on the floor trying to shake it off.

Slick watched in amazement as the dope fiends battled for control. If Jay pulled this off, he would reward him handsomely with a couple of rocks. His hopes were crushed when he saw Isis come out of nowhere, charging like a football player. She tackled Jay. It knocked him on his back. She grabbed him by his head and banged it to the floor until his arms went limp. Jay laid there bleeding from the back of his head. Michelle went over and helped Isis off top of him. Both breathed loudly. They should have tied Jay up. They had underestimated him because he was a drugged out doorman. The same way Slick and Smooth had under estimated them.

"I bet you were cheering for him, huh?" Michelle asked Slick.

Isis went over to get her pipe. "Damn, that mutha fucka made me break my pipe."

Slick managed weak smile. Isis looked at him. "Smile all you want. That shit won't happen no mo. I'll be ready the next time. If there is a next."

She and Michelle checked each others scratches and bruises from their battle with Jay. Once that was done they stood side by side. Isis heard the noise and Michelle saw Jay charge with what had to be her knife. Both women drew their guns and fired almost at the same time. The guns bucked in their small hands. Bullets tore through Jay's body, pushing him back by the steps. He crumbled to the floor never to move on his own again. Slick looked on in terror at the two women as he witnessed the brutal and vicious execution. They were still blowing smoke, wide eyed with marble mouth, and guns now aimed at him.

***

The multiple gun shots were heard upstairs. The big woman looked over her shoulder towards the bedroom door. She saw a dark tall figure standing by the door with his gun aimed in her direction. She screamed and pulled out of Smooth. She grabbed a sheet, attempting to cover her fat, sweat soaked, body. Smooth turned his head when he heard the shots. He looked around to see the man from the basement was watching him take it up the tail pipe.

Embarrassment, shame, and rage fueled his attempt to reach for his gun. Spook was just as surprised as they were to hear the shots from downstairs. Something had gone wrong. Now this big woman had seen him. Smooth lunged for his gun on the bedside table opposite the big woman who held the sheet to her breasts. Spook squeezed off two rounds. The .45 slugs found their way into Smooth's chest and head. His body jerked with each impact. His hand never reached his gun. The sound of the Desert Eagle bouncing off the four walls was deafening. The big woman was sprinkled with blood. She couldn't believe that fine ass Smooth lay a few feet from her dead. His eyes were still open.

Her instincts told her to try for the gun. Spook saw her look at the gun on the bed side table. "Do it and you die, here now!" he said in a cold voice.

"What do you want from me?" the big woman found enough nerve to say.

"You're coming downstairs with me. Come with the sheet. No time for your big ass to dress. Let's go. Now!"

She looked at back at the gun. Spook moved closer. He put his gun to her nose. "Move now bitch or gain some more weight with this lead."

She saw he was deadly serious. She was scared. Urine ran down her leg.

***

Michelle and Isis heard the gun shots from upstairs. They looked at each other and wondered if they should go investigate. They decided against it since Spook told them to stay put.

"Sound like your boy got a couple put in him," said Slick.

"Yeah, we'll see about that," replied Isis.

They heard footsteps coming down the steps. Isis and Michelle pointed their guns towards the stairs. Some big woman came down with Spook behind her, his gun to her head. Isis and Michelle smiled. Spook made big mama sit down on the floor by Slick in the piss puddle.

"What the fuck was that shooting about down here?" asked Spook as he viewed the doorman on the floor with blood escaping from holes in his chest.

Michelle answered, "Jay gave us some problems so Isis and I took good care of him."

"And we had to show this piece of shit some discipline," Isis said pointing her gun at Slick.

Spook looked at Slick and the blood crusting up around his feet. Spook was really digging these fresh out the gate gangsta bitches. A smile threatened his stone face.

"We had to show him that he ain't running shit here," Isis said. She walked over to her man, while he kept his gun on the big woman and Slick.

"We need to be going," said Spook.

"Just who in the fuck is this buffalo bitch?" asked Isis.

Spook said, "You wouldn't believe it. She had a strap on and was fucking Smooth with it." Michelle and Isis couldn't help but to laugh.

"Where is Smooth?" asked Slick.

"This black mutha fucka shot him down like a dog," said the big woman.

"Y'all sons of bitches don't know what y'all done did," said Slick, nodding his head towards the huge woman. "She and her brother ain't no small town dealers. Somebody gonna answer for this shit."

Hearing Slick say that gave the big woman some nerves. "Yeah, all y'all better find some rock to crawl under cause ain't no dope fiends gonna jack me and live to tell about it. Me and my brother supply more than half of these houses in this hick ass town," warned the big woman. "Just how in the hell did y'all know about this shipment tonight anyway?"

"And just who the fuck are you fat ass gorilla looking bitch?" said Isis.

"They call me Big Mama. You better recognize and ask somebody. You thin ass crack hoe. Put that gun down and I'll fuck yo dope fiend ass up bitch!"

Isis handed Michelle her gun, but as a true dope fiend kept her broken pipe in her hand and ran towards Big Mama.

Noooooo!" yelled Michelle.

Big Mama threw the sheet that was around her to the floor. She stood like a bear with outreached claws. It was comical because the strap on dick was still attached to her body. Isis ran into Big Mama hoping to knock her over, but it was to no avail. She didn't even move the big woman. The giant just grabbed Isis by her neck with both hands and lifted her from the floor.

Spook thought to himself, "If nothing else, this small bitch has heart."

Isis felt her air getting cut off from her brain. She started to slip into darkness. Spook and Michelle aimed their guns at the woman, but didn't shoot for fear of hitting Isis. Then something happened that not even Big Mama expected. Isis arched her back and extended her hands back as though yawning. With all her remaining strength, Isis slashed the jagged edge of her broken crack pipe across the big woman's neck. Blood gushed all over Isis giving Isis the appearance of something evil. Big Mama saw her blood and panicked. She dropped Isis to the floor hard and reached for the gaping hole in her throat. Isis sat up from the floor breathing heavy taking in the air she was denied. Big Mama staggered backwards and fell over Slick. She lay there bleeding out while making gurgling sounds. Spook looked at Michelle. She knew what he meant. Aide and assist your girl. Michelle walked over to the big woman, "All of you dealers always putting down us who do smoke, you say crack kills. The crack pipe killed you. Oh and by the way, don't you ever put your meat hooks on my wifey again. You uncomfortable built bitch."

Michelle balled her face and squeezed the trigger, putting a round in the woman's heart. Then Michelle walked over to Slick. He was looking at her when she aimed the gun at his head. He didn't want to die, not here on this floor. "Please don't do…" were his last words before Michelle shot him in the head.

Spook and Isis looked at this woman who had developed a blood lust like their own. Michelle looked at them both saying, "My mother used to say, if you're in for a penny, you're in for a pound."

The three of them went through the house looking for any liquids that would ignite. They found alcohol and all sorts of flammable liquids throughout the house. They poured it everywhere they could in a short time and set fire to it. The fire destroyed evidence of their presence. Flames could be seen through the windows of the house. The three never looked back as they hurried to the waiting black van with two duffel bags.

CHAPTER 12

Stone and Allen left from meeting with their lawyer and some local leaders of the community. They had been putting together a project for a month. The two were working out the details to open a youth center. A place that would have activities, literature, camping trips, sports, arts, music, all positive things to encourage the young mind. This would hopefully detour most from trouble on the streets. So far, everything looked good. The lawyer would get back with them once all the t's were cross and all the i's were dotted. It felt good knowing that they would be giving back to the community. Future plans included a car lot.

They were in Carol and Tomorrow's beauty shop getting groomed, talking, and laughing when a disturbing news report came on the T.V. The newscaster said a house had been shot up on Kendall Street. The details were sketchy, but four people were killed inside what appeared to be a dope house. It was a robbery or dope deal gone wrong. Three of them were out of Detroit.

Stone's jaw dropped. He got up from his manicure and paced the floor back and forth with his hand on his chin in deep thought. People noticed that he seemed uneasy.

"What's the matter baby?" asked Tomorrow.

Stone was so deep in thought, he didn't hear a word she said. Allen came from his chair walked behind Stone. Stone still in his pacing mode turned, almost running into Allen.

"What's up with you mellow?" asked Allen.

125

Stone realized he had made a scene then said, "I need to speak with all of you alone."

Carol and Tomorrow had their workers take over the shop for the rest of the day. The four of them left the shop and walked over to the girls' house. They sat in the living room waiting to hear what Stone had to say. All eyes were on Stone.

"Did you all hear the news flash about the drug house that got shot up with the four people getting killed?" asked Stone.

Tomorrow was sitting across Stone's lap, Allen and Carol were hugged up, and all of them were on the couch. "Yeah," was the answer they gave in unison.

"Well Tylor, also known as Big Mama, was from Detroit. Most of her family had been in the dope game for years. It's safe to say they've set up shop here in Battle Creek," explained Stone.

Everyone was thinking about it, but Allen went ahead and said it. "So what?"

"Well on the news they said Big Mama, whose real name is Kim Tylor, was killed in that house. Kim has a brother named Herbert Willie Tylor."

They all looked at Stone, still not getting it, waiting for the punch line. "It's a tragedy those people getting killed, but why has all this upset you so?" asked Tomorrow.

126

"Yes Stone. It's plain to see you're not your usual self," added Carol.

"And you've called us all in here for a hush, hush meeting. Why do you have the look of trouble in the making?" asked Allen.

Stone said, "Let me see if I can make it any plainer for you all. Big Mama is Herbert Willie Tylor's sister. We all had a run in with him last week."

Tomorrow, Carol, and Allen looked at one another. "We did? When?"

"Herbert Willie Tylor, is also known as Herbert T." Stone revealed.

Silence hung in the room as each of them reflected on their encounter with Herbert T. at the bar.

"I would definitely say trouble is in the making. I told you his family is into the drug trade strong. I'm sure him, his cousins, and who knows who else Herbert T, will bring here to get revenge," explained Stone.

"Yeah, I see what you're getting at. We are bound to run into him somewhere down the line, especially in a town of this size," said Allen.

Just then Allen's phone rang. He walked away from the others for privacy and answered it.

"Honey, you really think they will come here looking for trouble?" asked Tomorrow.

"The Herbert T I knew would. Then I could be wrong, but it's always a good idea to play it safe," answered Stone.

"That's true. One can never be too safe," said Tomorrow while planting a kiss on his lips.

"All the more reason why I'm going to start back carrying my little gun. Tomorrow, you should carry that .32 hand gun Stone bought for you a while back," reasoned Carol.

"Carol, you know I'm not much for guns. I haven't carried that thing since you gave it to me Stone."

"Carol's right baby. He's seen all of your faces, so at least have it handy until we know what's going on. I'll be carrying mine. I'd rather be tried by twelve, then to be carried by six. Besides it's better to have and not need, then to need and not have."

Before Tomorrow could respond, they heard Allen shouting, "I'm not finished talking to you yet!" Everyone looked in his direction. "No, don't hang up! Damn!"

Allen was angry. He put his cell phone back into his pocket. All of them looked at Allen with concern as he looked down at the floor, shaking his head.

Carol went to his side and grabbed his hand, "What's the matter baby?"

Stone said in a slow soft voice, "Mellow, tell us what's happened?"

Allen collected his composure before saying, "That was Spook bragging about how he just hit a nice lick and got paid. Then he asked me if I seen his handy work on the news. When I asked him what he talking about, he told me him and his crew took out some dope boys and some woman."

"He whaaaaat?" said Stone.

"He wants to make a name for himself by taking over some of these underworld businesses. He doesn't care who has to step on to pull himself up," explained Allen.

"Baby, has your brother gone crazy? He wants people to know? Don't he think whoever these dope dealers are will get the police involved?" asked Carol.

"Not necessarily true. Most dope dealers don't report such a thing. They seek their own street justice. So if Spook doesn't have any evidence pointing towards him, they won't help them with the investigation. On the other hand the police sometimes like this sort of thing, black on black crime, and it saves them some time and some bullets," added Stone.

They all knew this to be true.

"Yeah, but the fact still remains that Spook has lost his mind and he's out there ziggity boom," Tomorrow chimed in.

"I have no idea what to do. Those killings went down not far from one of our places. When Herbert T. and his minions start asking people questions, our names bound to come up. Closing our places down won't help because

Stone and I are well known around here. I just don't want any of us caught up in my brother's madness."

"Well the best we can do at the moment is take precautions and prepare ourselves. And may God help us not get hurt on this one," said Stone.

"Hey, why don't we all pack up and leave for a while? I know running isn't the answer, but we could just leave until some of the heat dies down. Carol and I have some money put away of our own," suggested Tomorrow.

"That's really not a bad idea Bee Spit. You and I could get married while we're away. Allen could be my best man and Carol could be your maid of honor. Nothing too fancy. We could book that flight to the Virgin Islands we've all been talking about. What do you think baby?"

Tomorrow was shocked beyond belief. She planted a big kiss on his lips, put her arms around his neck, and squeezed hard.

"Yes is the answer to your question. You know I will Stone. You just made me a very happy woman."

"I think that's a great idea. You two are made for each other," added Carol.

"Spook is my brother. I can't help but to be concerned for him. The last time I saw him he made it painfully clear that he would even hurt me if I got in his way. I told him about Herbert T. All Spook did was laugh, saying he'll take Herbert T. out worse than his sister. I told him he's put us all in harm's way. His response was if you want an omelet

130

you must break some eggs. Then he said he'd call me back and hung up on me. Spook knows what he's doing is wrong. Count me in. He's on his own for now. I wouldn't miss this for the world."

"I'm sure you girls have plenty to take care of before we leave. I need to call my mother and put her on a flight down south to her native soil. She can visit some of her old friends. How about everyone spend the rest of the day taking care of their business. Tonight we'll have a drink at Club Establishment and leave the first thing in the morning. What do you all think?" asked Stone.

Everyone agreed, although they also knew that things didn't often go as planned.

CHAPTER 13

They made it to the hotel room. Spook told them that all had earned their keep. Michelle and Crack Pipe had known each other for some time when her and Isis were wifey's. Spook asked Crack Pipe if he'd like Isis and Michelle to find him some female company. Crack Pipe refused the offer. When he smoked, he had a problem keeping it up. No matter how good looking or hot the female was, his shit just wouldn't respond so he stuck to getting high.

"Fine by me," said Spook while opening the door to the joining hotel room. "Me and the girls will be over here getting our freak on." Spook left Crack Pipe a small mountain of crack on the table so he could smoke at will.

"Now don't hurt yourself, I don't need you overdosing. Too much of this shit will bust your heart. You gonna be alright?" asked Spook.

Crack Pipe was too high to talk so he just nodded his head.

"And remember what I said. Try and eat something. I'll leave you a couple of these burger's we stopped and got on the way here. Oh, and drink some of that liquor or beer to take the edge off a bit. I mean look at you man. All of us have taken showers and you're still sweating like a government mule. I'll have one of the girls check on you later. I want us all to get a couple hours of sleep."

The girls had already started without Spook. Spook watched them as he undressed. They were buck booty naked on the bed smoking crack and weed taking turns blowing smoke on each other's pussies while fingering themselves. Spook thought to himself how his new life style was starting to pay off. Free money, free drugs, free girls. Hell, that's the American dream! He smiled.

Isis tasted the fingers she had just removed from her pussy.

"I've been meaning to ask you, why do you taste your own pussy? I think it's sexy and all but why do you do that?" asked Spook. He was standing over the girls naked. Isis was in her zone and when she spoke her voice came out in whispers.

"Because I like it. Would you like to taste me? I'm clean inside just for you." asked Isis. She went back to playing with herself.

"Bitch, I don't eat pussy. The last time I ate some pussy was when I was birthed coming out of one. Don't you ever invite my face to that shit. I'm strictly dickly, you got that?" said Spook squinting his eyes at her.

"Yeah I'm okay with that. Don't get mad at me baby. I just want to please my man."

"Well right now one of y'all can please me with a weenie wash."

Michelle was fingering herself even harder and faster while her blue eyes were locked and fixated on his long thick penis. "Oh yes. Climb in here with us big daddy. Let me slob on Bob." Michelle said.

"Crawl to it, like a big cat and lick it like a kitty cat licks milk," said Spook. He was aroused and aimed himself at Michelle. He stood at the edge of the bed. Michelle crawled on all fours to the end of the bed. Spook was still standing when she grabbed his member and began circling her tongue and licking it like a cat licks milk. Isis scooted beneath Michelle and pulled her ass down so Michelle's pussy was in her face. Michelle was so into it. She ran her tongue up and down his shaft.

Isis licked Michelle's special spot while rubbing and tapping her own. Sounds of pleasure filled the room. It felt good to Spook. He placed his hands behind her head. He knew his nails pressed in the creases of her ears kept the woman at that very spot. If she pulled back, his finger nail would cause much pain.

"Suck that dick. Just like that. Yeah suck that dick. You gonna swallow all that shit. Suck it. Yeah just like that. Suck it!"

Humming and slurping sounds could be heard. He let out a groan. Then she felt the hot stream of sperm hitting the back of her neck. He let her go and flopped down on the bed and watched the women do their thing. Michelle was still in doggie style position. Her legs were wide open and Isis was below her being very busy. Isis thumped Michelle's clit with her tongue. Michelle shook uncontrollably as shock waves went through her body.

"Damn, your mouth feels so good on me," whispered Michelle.

Spook had regained his sex drive and couldn't stand it any longer. Watching them really turned him on.

He put his wand into Isis. He felt his dick being swallowed by her wet waiting pussy. Isis began to hum as she anticipated her climax. Spook took hard and long strokes. He dug in and out of her.

Michelle reached her climax. "Oh ....Oh ..oh I'm there...Oh shit." She grabbed the sheets. Her eyes opened wide as she felt the wetness going down her legs. She rolled to the side of them and watched Isis take all of that dick. Michelle massaged her own her breast while sucking Isis' breast. She enjoyed the sight of Isis getting dicked down. They had been at it for along time.

"Fuck that pussy baby...fuck that pussy.... Yeah....Yeah, fuck that pussy....fuck it baby....Oh, here it comes," cried Isis.

Spook increased his tempo, "Give it to me. You good pussy bitch you."

Isis came back to back. She gave in to what this man thrusted in and out of her. Spook came right behind her growling like some animal. When he finished, he rolled to her side. She laid there with her legs open staring at the ceiling. Both were breathing hard.

"My turn big daddy, give me that hot beef injection," Michelle said.

Spook was pussy drunk but he had to give Michelle some dick. He reached over Isis and grabbed the bottle of

Hennessey. He took a long drink then turned back to Michelle handing her the bottle.

She took a drink and sat it back down on the bed side table. The liquor warmed her body as it coursed its way through her. She laid flat on her back and opened her legs again. She played with her pussy. This made Spook ready again. He got between her legs and entered her slowly. She watched his black dick as it entered her white pussy. She grabbed his ass and hurried him to go deep. She felt every inch of him. Michelle's mouth flew open displaying her white teeth. She was prey that had been caught by a predator.

"Damn, you're so huge. Dick me down baby, damn, damn, damn," breathed Michelle.

She threw her legs up in the air. Spook worked with it as Michelle absorbed each of his thrusts. The pussy was good to him. Spook couldn't hold it much longer so he went faster giving her all he had left. He beared all his weight down with each powerful thrust. The bed springs squeaked in protest.

"Oh my goodness ….. Oh my goodness, Oh ……Oh….. Oh…. " cried Michelle.

"You like this dick …Huh …You …Like this dick…Don't you bitch?"

She really did enjoy the way he was beating up her pussy. "Oh yeah… Fuck me…This dick is so good I want you to break it off … Inside me…fuck ..Meeeeeeeee," screamed Michelle. She bucked below him like a gazelle. She felt him all through her body as she began to shake when she came. She reached multiple orgasms for the first time in her life. She dug her nails into his buttocks and just held on tight. It seemed like she couldn't stop cumming as he continued to stab her pussy. She threw her head from side to side, inhaled deeply and screamed at a very high pitch, "Aaaaaaaaaaaaahhhhhh."

Then Spook let go. His sperm mixed with her fluids. Michelle's legs went down and she collapsed under him. She laid there with her body jerking from time to time. She experienced muscle spasms from the increased pleasure.

Isis sat up. She looked at Spook who was on his back lighting a cigarette, then she looked at Michelle. "Damn baby, you fucked her into a coma."

Spook sat up to take a good look at Michelle. She was out cold with a big smile on her face. She was sleeping like a new born baby in the fetal position. "You think she's gone be okay?"

"Yeah, she'll be fine. Her pussy will be sore, like mine, but she'll be just fine. She probably hasn't slept or ate right in days. That is not to take anything away from the dick though. I'm sure she's like me, haven't ever been dicked down like that before. She's a good wifey, can she stay with us baby?"

"Yeah, she can. Go check on your brother. Tell him to shut down and get a few hours of sleep. I'm taking all of you out later tonight."

Isis checked on Crack Pipe then came back to bed. She cuddled up with Spook and Michelle. Isis went to sleep with Spook's manhood in her hand.

They woke up hours later. Crack Pipe was doing his tweak thing. Spook had everyone take showers and sent the girls out for supplies, clothes, and food. He cut Crack Pipe off from getting high so he could drive.

Later, he had the girls take a cab to pick up his car. He had parked it before buying the van. The girls returned. They looked good in fresh gear. Spook fought back the urge to go another round with them. The girls had everything he asked them to pick up. Now the girls and Crack Pipe wanted to get high. Spook told them only after everyone got some food in their stomachs. They could smoke weed because it would help their appetites. They all protested.

Spook reminded them with warning under tones in his deep voice, "I'm the captain of this ship and I'll sail it or sink it. You all need some guidance and discipline. Now if anyone here has a problem with that, they can do the Michael Jackson and beat it.

"I don't mind any of you getting high. Hell, I do it myself, but there is a time for everything. When we're on a mission or preparing for one, I don't need any of you zombie out and stuck on stupid. You must eat in order to keep up your strength and it helps you to think straight. I'll treat all of you good. Just don't violate any of my rules. We are a family and I want you all to treat each other as family. It's us against the world. I tell you this out of love."

He had their undivided attention. Spook went into the rest room. He gave them time to allow his words to sink in. Isis admired Spook. She looked at him through love struck eyes. The three reasoned among themselves. They agreed that Spook was right. He was only looking out for them. No one they knew in this dope game gave a damn about their welfare.

Although he was brutal and vicious at times, he gave them all the dope they needed with shelter and food. Plus they partied and he looked out for them. He only asked that they didn't get so high when the family was into something. Weighing Spook on a scale pound for pound, they fared better with him than with any involved in the game from their past. Yes, he had a cruel side, but only if you didn't do what he said. Spook was the lesser of two evils, besides they all were a family now, which gave them a sense of belonging and being accepted. They would be content with smoking weed, for now, anyway.

Spook let them think that he was using the rest room. He held his head to the door and listened to them reason about him cutting off their get high for now. Back in the day, he was a master pimp. He dealt with women on a constant basis. He liked this new crew. They just needed some of his fine tuning. If it wasn't for the money and dope, he'd have all of them on the stroll, including Crack Pipe.

Spook had to know if they were really in his corner. He wanted to trust them, but he had to be sure. Spook learned a long time ago that when drugs came into play everything could be going just fine then people within your circle will flip the script for whatever reason. The game will change

139

dramatically when sabotage, espionage, mutiny, and high treason enter the picture. All of which are punishable by death for hundreds of years. The second one of them showed the slightest hint of flipping the script, he'd kill them dead. Hearing them reason among themselves and agreeing that he was looking out for them made him smile and unbeknown to them saved their lives. They passed his test. Spook flushed the toilet, opened the door, and headed out to join them with a thick blunt hanging from his mouth still lit.

CHAPTER 14

It was evening. The winds were low and there was some snow still on the ground. The streets were cleared by the big shoveled trucks and salt was put on the treacherous icy streets of Battle Creek. There had been a mild ice storm earlier that morning. The trees were covered with ice. They gave off beautiful colors as the sun hit the ice. The streets looked dingy white in some places from the salt residue. A powder blue Hummer with dark tinted windows pulled up to the curb. Four men exited the vehicle. Each man wore were expensive shoes along with tailor made suits and long coats. They made it to the door of the building that once was a small furniture store.

S & A Pool Hall was written in big letters. The four men entered the building. One of the men stood by the door while the other three continued walking to the counter. A fat, balding man with a thick cigar hanging from his mouth sat there. Ashes from the cigar had fallen and rested on his protruding stomach. At the sight of the four men, he stood, ashes now fell from his stomach to the floor.

The place held ten pool tables. Only five were being used while a few more people stood around talking. Gambling of all sorts went on in the back room.

"Yes can I help you?" asked the fat man behind the counter. Immediately he noticed the bulges under the men's suit coats. Each man undid the buttons on their coats.

The one with the look of authority spoke, "I'd like to know, does Stone own this Place?"

The fat balding old man behind the counter felt trouble in the making. He had never seen any of these four men before. They looked suspicious. He didn't live to be sixty years old by being a fool. Something was up. He didn't know what, but something was definitely up.

"Yeah, this is his place," answered the old man.

"I want you to give him an important message for me."

The balding man stood there, taking a long drag from his cigar. His first instinct was to press the button under the counter to alert those people who were in the back gambling, this could be a stick up. Then he quickly dismissed the stick up theory, these men before him were farting through silk, dressed to kill. Hopefully he wouldn't be the one getting killed. He cursed himself for not pushing the button when he could without drawing attention to himself. To do so now might get him hurt or even killed.

"Tell him Herbert T. is in town. I just came from putting my sister in the ground. I need some answers and soon. Word on the streets is he knows who killed her or he's connected to her killer somehow. Here's my cell number. It's imperative that you give him my message. You feel me old times?" He placed a piece of paper with his cell number on it inside the man's shirt pocket, and then he reached up taking the cigar from the man's mouth.

"You will tell him, right?" asked Herbert T.

"Yeah. Yeah, yes of course," said the fat bald man. Sweat gathered on his forehead.

"Now if I don't hear from Stone in a matter of a few hours, I'll be back. I'm sure you wouldn't like that because it would be very unhealthy for you. So it's important for you and me that he gets this message, so I can count on you right?"

"Yes sir, I'll tell him myself."

"Good , you do just that," said Herbert T. Then he dropped the cigar he had taken from the old man's mouth and crushed it out with the heel of his shoe. He turned and walked out with the three men close behind him. The fat man wiped the sweat from his forehead and let out a sigh of relief when the door closed behind them. He picked up the phone to call Stone or Allen. It didn't matter which one, but it was his sole mission to deliver the message.

***

"What the hell that high yellow bitch got that I don't Stone?" yelled Delsena.

"Del, I've never heard your mouth to be so foul before," said Stone.

They were sitting on the couch, she was wearing a robe. "Well, it's not every day that the man you love tells you he's marrying some other woman. So, hell yeah, I'm pissed off. It would be nice if we could just hold hands and sing kum-bye-ya, but we both know it isn't a perfect world and life throws things at you. I'm only human Stone."

Stone sat there fully dressed with his coat still on. He left Allen so the both of them could tie down any loose ends before leaving the following day. Stone decided he must go over to Del's house and let her know what was up. He bought her up to date on current events, concerning Herbert T., his sister's death, and Spook. Then he dropped the bombshell on her about him and Tomorrow getting married soon. Delsena was worried about Stone and this Herbert T. He had come too far to get pulled back into that kind of life. Stone assured her not to worry. It would be handled, so they went on to talk about him and Tomorrow.

He loved them both. His feelings had been torn between the two ladies for some time now. Stone found himself loving them both for different reasons. Both were strong women. Both were self contained. He knew both of them loved him as well and both were wonderful in bed. Sex isn't the most important thing in a relationship, but it is important. Whoever says it isn't, has issues that need tissues.

Del and Stone both believed she couldn't give Stone a family. She had tried having children earlier but without success. It had something to do with her being raped by her relatives when she was only fourteen. She was now in her early thirties with a young woman's body and a good head on her shoulders. A beautiful chocolate woman indeed.

Tomorrow, however, was in her late twenties, nice body, light skinned, and she could have children. She also had a good head on her shoulders. Tomorrow being able to give a Stone a family was the major deciding factor. Just the thought of Tomorrow's child bearing hips made him horny.

Stone snapped back to the present situation. Del was really angry. They'd always kept it real with one another, so it stood to reason that he owed Del the truth. "Baby, have no doubts about my love for you. I've wrestled with this decision on my head for months now. I'm ready to settle down and start a family. I'll always love you and you'll forever be a dear friend to me and always in my heart," he explained.

Delsena poked her sexy lips out and crossed her arms. "I'm not hating on her. If the truth be told, I like Tomorrow. She's the only one I allow to do my hair. I mean her girl Carol, looks to be good at what she does, but I like for Tomorrow to fix me up. She knows what you and I are to each other. She could easily sabotage my hair and nails. Yet, as long as I've been going there, she has always been professional, always courteous, and always polite. Plus, she does good work. She and Carol have dined at some of my restaurants on more than one occasion. I just draw the line where you're concerned."

They were at Delsena's house out on Beatle Lake Road. Stone loved coming way out here in this wooded area. Her house sat a good ways off in the woods from the main road. No sounds of traffic, no sirens, and no sounds of people cussing each other out could be heard. It was a healing quiet that he could really get used to. Delsena was a beautiful black woman. She had everything going for her, looks, money, she was intelligent, and she had her own mansion. She could have any man she wanted. She was man's dream, yet she was stuck on him. Damn, there was no denying that he loved her.

145

"Can I at the very least come to the wedding to give you both my blessings and show there is no hard feelings?" asked Delsena.

"Baby, I would like that. I think is commendable of you, but should know the marriage will be done while we're all away."

"Oh, well, you tell her I said congrats and give her my blessings, okay?" She reached for Stone, gave him a kiss and laid her head in his lap.

Stone was befuddled. "Why the quick change of heart? You were just pouting. Now you're smiling, what have you got on that wicked mind of yours?" He moved the top half of her robe to expose her breasts.

She wore nothing under the robe. He began to lightly rub her nipple. It responded to his touch, swelling upwards. She closed her eyes and enjoyed the feel of his hand on one of her erogenous zones.

"I'm not having a change of heart. I still stand adamantly by my decision. If I had my way, you'd be marrying me instead. It occurred to me that she won't keep you for long. I'm not burning bread on you or her. It just seems you and I were meant to be baby. When you two break up, I'll be there to pick up the pieces. Or when you get that itch, I'll be there to scratch it," said Delsena. She was sure of herself as she pulled him down to kiss her. She guided his hand to her wet vagina.

"Baby, I love you enough to ask that you move on with your life," replied Stone. He was getting hard. She reached down with both of her hands and placed them on his hand that was darting in and out of her love tunnel. She plunged his hand further inside her. She brought her hips to meet his hand. She sucked air in and out with short breaths until she climaxed.

She lay there making sexy cooing sounds. Stone removed his clothes. Delsena sat up on the couch and threw her robe to the side. She pulled him on top of her kissing him with urgency. She looked him square in the eyes and said, "Stone, you can think me to be a fool for it, but you are the love of my life. I truly love you. My mind is made up not to move on so why wait?" "I choose to wait on you." "I want you to move on, so why wait? "

She guided his hard member inside her, grabbed his rear with both hands, and pumped up and down. She felt his rod stiffen even more inside of her

Stone was grinding slow, looking down at this woman he had total respect for. She still had her eyes closed. She bit her lower lip. A tear escaped from her eye and ran down the side of her face. He felt ready to release his load. He fought back the feelings.

"Del, why won't you answer me?" he breathed.

"Because a wise man once told me, it is better to be thought a fool than to open your mouth and remove all doubt."

"Who told you that?" asked Stone.

She was throwing it at him. He lost all control. Stone quickened his pace while still looking down at her.

His veins popped out of his neck and forehead as he deposited his load in her womb. Delsena felt the rush of his fluids. Her eyes shot open as she pulled him so his chest was flush with her breasts and his ears was close to her mouth. Then she came, and whispered, "It …Was…..Youuuuuuuuuuu."

Stone and Delsena showered and changed into new dress gear. Delsena kept a closet just for Stone. It was stocked with shirts, pants, suits, jewelry, shoes, belts, ties, socks, underwear, and cologne. She really put love into everything she did for Stone. They went to one of Del's restaurants in separate cars. She had a limo with a female driver, but Delsena opted to drive herself around most of the time.

Delsena arrived a little before Stone. He parked beside her. She had her own space with her name on it. Stone hadn't been here in a while. The place was elegant. It had real cotton napkins and cotton tablecloths. They were seated in the V.I.P. selection, overlooking the lake. The manager and chef came over and gave salutations to their boss and owner along with Stone. They sipped on cognac by candlelight.

Stone wore a white tailor made suit with a canary yellow shirt. His hair was brushed back into a ponytail. His jewelry consisted of a blue diamond pinky ring, and matching cuff links, a Rolex, and a gold bracelet that dangled about his wrist, accenting his watch. Delsena was the Belle of the Ball. She wore her long black hair down and a black dress that exposed her back clear down to her waist line. The dress was cut high in the front with spaghetti straps. It showed off her cleavage and beautiful mahogany skin.

She also wore stilettos, a diamond ankle bracelet that was embedded in platinum, yellow diamonds intertwined with blue sapphires hung on her neck and her earrings were white diamond tear drops. She was so iced up that when the lights shined on her jewelry, it gave the effect of tiny lights exploding around her.

"You look so lovely tonight Delsena." He said.

"Thank you. You look dashing yourself. However, I'm not pleased with my hair."

"Baby, you look wonderfully amazing. I don't see how your hair could look any better."

"Well I do!"

"How?" asked Stone, downing the rest of his drink.

"My hair would look much better between your legs."

Stone had to laugh. He caught the little bit of drink he laughed back up with his napkin. Del laughed with him and patted his back in case he choked. "You okay?"

Stone cleared his throat and composed himself. "Yeah. I'm alright. When you said that, I pictured your head down there. You caught me totally off guard with that one."

"Stoney," she said with her voice full of pleasure, "I'm really going to miss the times we've shared. I want you to give me your word that you'll always remain in contact with me. I'll always and forever be there for you. It's important to me that you believe that."

Stone was feeling what she said. All he could do for the moment was look at this woman who taught him more than he cared to admit. "Delsena, what I say comes from my heart. You have been, and always will be, a special person in my life. You've helped me grow in areas I didn't even know I had. You were there when no one else was. You've always believed in me. For that I'm eternally grateful. You've given me balance when I was unstable.

What I feel for you cannot be measured in words. I love you. I'll always love you. Yes, I'll keep in contact. If you ever need me, I will be there."

Their eyes locked for a moment, she placed her hand on his. The rest of their dinner engagement went well. When it was time for Stone to leave, he walked her to her car. They kissed, hugged, and said their goodbyes. Stone drove away.

Delsena sat in her car and listened to the sounds of Mary J. Blige. Tears welled up in her eyes and she had herself a good cry. She missed Stone already.

CHAPTER 15

Stone turned his phone off because he wanted his last moments with Delsena to be undisturbed. As he drove down Capital Avenue, he checked for messages. He had two messages. One from Allen and the other from the pool hall. He called Allen first.

Allen told him about Herbert T's visit. Stone told Allen to strap up and meet him at his house. Allen already had his gun on him and would be at Stone's house in fifteen minutes. Allen was in his driveway when Stone arrived. They went inside and Allen told Stone all he knew. Stone took out twin .357 Mag. Pythons and a holster belt made for the twins that hid them neatly at the small of his back. Allen's gun of choice was a .44 auto mag. His shoulder holster was under his coat.

"You set?" asked Allen.

"Yeah, let's go."

Everything was pretty quiet when they arrived at the pool room. The only people there were the ones who worked for Stone and Allen. After Herbert T's visit, Allen had them close up shop. The fat man told Stone the details about Herbert T's visit. He gave Stone the card that Herbert T. left for him. They told their workers to take a week off with pay and to lock everything up. Stone and Allen rode around town looking for the powder Blue Hummer. There couldn't be that many in this town, if any at all.

Allen looked over at Stone, who was driving. "What are we going to do when we find them?" Allen asked.

"Hopefully, just talk and come up with a peaceful resolution."

"I know you want to find out where he is before you call him, but maybe we should just call him."

"Yeah, I was just thinking the same thing." Stone let out a deep breath.

They pulled into Club Establishment's parking lot. Stone pulled out his phone and punched in the number on the card that Herbert T had left for him. The phone rang five times before someone answered. "Run yo mouth."

"This is Stone. I understand you wanted to talk to me."

"Stoney Boy, I'm glad you got back at me. I've taken care of the necessary arrangements of putting my sister away properly and I'm here in town to take care of some unfinished business. You remember my sister Kim don't you? I remember her telling me that she tricked with you a few times."

"Yes, I remember Big Mama."

She would pay Stone drugs for sex. It came to a screeching halt when she tried sticking her finger up his ass. Stone didn't care how much dope she gave him, her finger or anything else wasn't going up his ass. He remembered telling Big Mama, that his ass was just a one way street.

"Let me extend my most sincere condolences. May God bless her soul. Listen Herbert T. about our last meeting..."

152

Herbert T. interrupted him, "It's forgotten Stoney Boy, I was out of line for that. I extend my apologies."

"Like you said, it's forgotten," Stone said with some reservations.

"The reason I needed to speak to you is I need your help. You see Stoney Boy, I'm on unfamiliar ground here. I was hoping you and I could meet. I don't trust phones for matters of a sensitive nature such as this. Just so you know that I'm on the up and up, we can meet anywhere of your choice."

"Give me some time to think about it. I'll call you back in a couple of hours."

"Stoney Boy, I can't express how much this means to me. I really need you to come through for me on this one. I'll be waiting to hear from you."

The line went dead. Stone told Allen what was said.

"Things have gotten very complicated," said Allen.

"Yeah, I still don't know how I'm going to play it. From experience I know that Herbert T. is not that cordial. He doesn't apologize to anyone. There are too many unknown factors, variables we're not fully aware of. I'm sure he wants who did this to his sister, but at the same time it could be a trap.

"You are like a brother to me. Yet it's your brother he wants. It's no secret that I don't care much for Spook, but he's your brother and I know if something happened to him you'd be hurting. I just can't allow that to happen. I'm still at square one," said Stone. He was perplexed.

"I don't like Spook or what he's doing. I'll always love him because he's my brother. He's my flesh and blood."

"I'm feeling that. Blood is thicker than mud."

"I'm surprised he hasn't found out it was Spook that did his sister. The street grapevine has Spook's name ringing all around town. It's just a matter of time before it reaches Herbert T. or the police," said Allen.

"I'm not sure it hasn't already. I mean the police have people on the streets. Herbert T. has his connections. This whole thing may be the overlay for underplay. This might be calm before the storm. For all we know, Herbert T. or the police could be closing in all around us as we speak," said Stone. He did not mean to make Allen uneasy.

Allen turned his head and looked around from the passenger seat. He expected Herbert T. or the police to materialize from nowhere. A bit of paranoia set in.

"I agree. It would be a big mistake to rule that out. People gossip and run their mouths all the time. The three fastest ways for news to travel is telephone, telegraph, and the streets," said Allen to bring a bit of comic relief to their grave situation.

Stone smiled and came back at him, "Above all, we must keep our wits about us. Paranoia will destroy ya." Stone added his own comic relief and realism at the same time.

154

"So what's next?"

"I'm not sure yet. Although your brother Spook rubs me the wrong way, I won't give him up to Herbert T. I am sure that Herbert T will remain in town until he gets what he wants. I mean whatever decision we make affects us both."

"True that. Needless to say I'm with you to the end. We didn't build our small empire for Herbert T. to tear it down. Stone, you've always been the thinker of our operation. All I do is execute the plan and help finance whatever endeavors we see fit. I say we meet him and bring this to a head."

"Okay, meet him it is. We'll talk, but Spook's name doesn't come up," replied Stone.

"Agreed. I'll protect my brother and I appreciate your silence mellow."

They left the car and went in their club. It had gotten dark and people were just starting to come to Club Establishment. Stone and Allen went to the bar and both ordered drinks. They wanted to talk to Dwayne but he seemed to be nowhere to be found. They went to the club's back office. Dwayne wasn't there. The other workers said that Dwayne hadn't came in yet. Dwayne's second in charge said it was very unusual for Dwayne not to show up. If he was sick or needed some time off, they would have known about it. Dwayne was a workaholic.

Stone and Allen went to their private section to formulate a plan. The first thing was to figure out where to meet. Then they needed to figure out how to come out of this on top, instead of six feet under.

CHAPTER 16

Tomorrow and Carol were packing when the phone rang.

"Hello!" Tomorrow's sweet voice answered.

It was Veeda, one of the employees from the beauty shop, "Sorry to disturb you girl. I know you are preparing for your big trip and all, but I have these two big spenders out here. They say they don't want anyone doing their hair and nails but you. Girl, they paid me $50 just make sure I called you girl."

"Who are they?" asked Tomorrow.

"Girl, I've never seen them before, but they said Stone referred them."

"Well I guess I could. What could doing two more customers hurt?"

"So, what do I tell them?"

"Tell them I'll be there in ten," Tomorrow hung up the phone.

"What did Veeda want? asked Carol as she went about still packing.

"They have two big spenders who want my touch."

"Well you make it work. I can finish packing. Allen and Stone take longer then us getting ready for anything."

"Alright, don't forget to pack my Jewelry. If my baby comes, tell him to have a seat. I'll see you all before long."

"I won't forget your jewelry. I got you covered."

Tomorrow went to the rest room, fixed herself up a bit, and made her way to the shop. Two men she had never seen before stood from their chairs when she entered.

Veeda whispered in her ear, "That's them. They both look like they're paid but still have that thuggish look to me."

Tomorrow walked over to the men and used her professional voice, "How may I help you gentlemen?"

One man opened up his coat to reveal a gun. The other did the talking, "Don't be alarmed or make a scene. If you indicate to anyone what's up, my friend here will kill you and everyone in here."

Tomorrow was struck with fear.

"Now I have someone who wants to talk to you. So don't make us hurt you and all of these people. Just come with us. If you understand, nod your head," asked the nice dressed man with the bald head and beard.

The other man with the gun said, "Let's go!"

"It's cold out there. Can I at least grab my coat?" asked Tomorrow.

She was hoping she could alert Carol or anyone. She was scared and didn't know what to do. Things were happening too fast. The shop was so busy no one even noticed that she was being abducted.

"No. You will be just fine. We parked close to the door. Now move it!" said the man with the beard. He was losing his patience.

He grabbed her arm and herded her towards the door. Once they were all inside the vehicle, they took off. They sped away from the beauty shop, having carried out Herbert T's orders.

***

Spook had been with Isis, Michelle and Crack Pipe for a few days now. They had been getting high, eating, sleeping, and fucking. Not always in that order. He was good and rested. Crack Pipe hadn't spoken for a whole day. They never thought they could have so much fun or get so high until Spook came along. They even hit a couple of clubs out of town, partying the night away. Crack Pipe would sit at the table with Spook while the girls danced together. Despite Spook's ruthlessness, they really liked this dark killer who protected them. Fast food containers were all over the tables and floors in the both hotel rooms. Spook had a routine. Every day they had to eat and shower twice a day. Even Crack Pipe showered without being told. Spook was bored with it, so he told them that the honeymoon was over. It was time for them to go back to work. With what he had and one more good lick, he could put people to work for him on a big scale. He could buy his very own place and really start running things. Spook and Crack Pipe were at the table getting high and the girls were the bed naked. They took turns sucking their pipes and sucking on each other.

"Don't you bitches ever get tired of sucking on each other?" asked Spook.

Crack Pipe's speech was getting better while high, he managed to say, "Isis is loony and that damn Michelle is way out there. That's why they get along so well."

"Shut up Crack Pipe. You know well dope makes us horny. Just cause yo ass chooses to tweak instead of freak is on you. Spook come and join us baby," said Isis.

Crack Pipe cut in, "I may choose to tweak instead of freak but at least I ain't crazy. You're crazier then Chicken Little. That mutha fucka thought the sky was falling."

"Both y'all shut up. You mutha fucka's giving me a headache. I won't join you. I just told y'all the honeymoon is over. Now get y'all ass over here and lets formulate our next move," demanded Spook.

The girls stopped what they were doing and sat at the table with Spook and Crack Pipe. Spook asked what other dope spot would make a good target. They threw a few names out but discarded them because most, if not all ,the spots in the hood knew about houses getting jacked. They would be prepared.

Then Michelle had an idea. She told them about these white dealers she knew who stayed way out in the sticks around Kalamazoo. It was only about twenty miles from Battle Creek. Michelle lived in Kalamazoo so she knew the area well. Hopefully, they wouldn't know much about what went on in Battle Creek.

This got Spook's total attention. It was a great idea. She said these dope dealers rarely sold crack. Their thing was mostly crystal meth, weed, and some heroin from time to time. Spook asked for specifics. How many dealers? How far away? What kind of guns did they have? How much weight did they sell? Could she get them in the dealer's house to make a buy?   She gave favorable answers to most of his questions. Some answers she wasn't sure. Spook felt the fox was worth the chase.

"Okay, y'all get yourselves ready, and no more getting high for now. Isis and Michelle pack up all our paraphernalia. We're getting a new hotel. We've been here long enough. We'll get a new room first. After the job we can go straight to the room and lay low.

"Crack Pipe take these keys and this money. Get us two joining rooms on the opposite side of town, out near the high way. Gas up the van. Oh, make sure you get some cigarettes and hurry back."

Crack Pipe pulled himself together and went to complete his tasks. The girls were still naked, but they picked up and put things away.

Michelle bent over in front of Spook. "Damn this bitch," Spook thought to himself as her voluptuous ass cheeks spread open like a flower in bloom. He felt himself grow hard. Isis didn't make it any better by leaning over him while he sat at the table. Her nipples brushed his face while she grabbed things from the table.

"These bitches know exactly what they're doing," he thought, "Now that Crack Pipe is gone, they're tag teaming me." Isis went over by Michelle and was bending over the same way. Spook stood and undid his pants. He could have sworn he heard them giggling softly. They watched him through open legs while bent over as he approached.

CHAPTER 17

Michelle wasn't lying. This place was far out in a rural area. The snow had melted and the ground was dry. It turned out to be a nice sunny day. They had traveled for some time before turning off on a back dirt road. They still weren't there yet. Spook, Isis, Michelle, and Crack Pipe had unloaded everything in their new rooms, including all their drugs. Spook didn't want to ride dirty to a mission.

Spook said, "Damn Michelle, this is way the fuck out in he sticks. You sure you know where you going?"

"Yeah baby, and I called him like you told me to. I told him I had good old friend who was in town for a while, I told him that you'd smoke a lot of the dope that he sells. He was all for that. Me and Isis may have to give a couple of them some head to get them relaxed so you can do yo thing. You okay with that?" Michelle replied.

Isis jumped in before Spook can answer, "Baby, I told her to ask you first, I don't want you mad."

"Nah, this is work. It ain't personal. Y'all do what you must," said Spook.

Michelle gave them a quick back ground on meth so they wouldn't be going in blind. "Marty is the head man. He'll more than likely have his boys Billy Bob and Chuck there too. They have a small meth lab in the back of the house.

"Most people have heard of Meth in forms of crank, speed, ice, and of course crystal meth. It's cheaper and the high lasts much longer then crack. When it's being made, the smell is loud. Let me see what else... Oh, I almost forgot, watch out for the meth monsters. They think they have bugs on their body and/or face. They pick on their skin until it bleeds and causes sores."

All of them listened to Michelle with interest as she continued, "Just like crack this shit makes people react differently. I knew this guy once who shaved off every hair on his body. Even his pubics and eyebrows. Then he pulled his eyelashes out so the bugs had nowhere to hide. But even after that, he would ask people if they saw any bugs on him. Those who can't handle it freak out in one way or another.

"There may be some people in Marty's back rooms. He lets users go back there to get high, get their freak on, or whatever, just as long as they are spending money with him. Some shoot meth, some put it into capsules and there are those who smoke it. It don't take much to get high depending on how it's made. It's high yield, so don't get greedy getting high on the shit. That's meth one-oh- one."

They traveled the rest of the way in silence. There was nothing but corn and wheat fields as far as the eye could see. The only movement other than some beat up trucks and a couple of tractors passing them on this back road from time to time was crows. They hadn't seen any of them for awhile.

"The house should be down this road around that next bend," Michelle pointed out the window.

Spook checked the load in his gun and then chambered a round. He placed his gun in its holster. Isis, wanted to be like her man and impress Spook at the same time. She copied him by checking her gun the same way he did.

"Stop the van!" Michelle screamed.

Crack Pipe slammed on the brakes, causing everyone in the van to be uprooted from their seats violently. The wheel kept Crack Pipe in place. The rest weren't as fortunate. The momentum caused them to crash into the back of the seats in front of them and the floor. The van's tires scraped up dust from the road. The dirty dust settled down on the van like a cloud.

"What the fuck did you tell him to do that for?" shouted Spook. He pulled himself off Isis who was on the floor. Michelle and Isis got up at the same time. Isis looked at Michelle like she had two heads.

"I'm sorry y'all, but when I saw you guys checking your weapons, something I forgot to tell you just hit me," Michelle said.

"Spook, do you want me to keep driving, or stay here in the middle of the road?" Crack Pipe interrupted.

"Get us out the middle of the damn road. Pull over to the side until this bitch explains herself," said Spook.

"I forgot a very important thing," said Michelle. She let out a long sigh and held her head down.

Isis was getting more pissed by the minute. She shouted, "Spit it out bitch!"

Michelle said, "I forgot to tell you that Marty is very paranoid. He'll probably check us for guns."

Crack Pipe pulled the van over to the side of the dirt road. He was glad someone else was being yelled at for a change. He added his two cents, "How in the hell could you forget some shit like that?"

"Do you see why I don't want anyone getting high a few hours before we make a move? Let this be a lesson to all you," said Spook. He was all up in Michelle's face pointing his finger at her. Then he continued, "I don't want to go in there without an edge. Michelle go sit your ass down away from me while I think how we can still do this."

Michelle went to the passenger seat. She was hurt because she felt she let her family down. Spook felt like going upside her head, but that wouldn't bring him any closer to the money and dope he needed to get his operation off the ground. He could always call the whole thing off and come up with something different.

They couldn't wait on this road long. Nothing but whites stayed this far back in the woods. The way he figured it, he was too black for their comfort level. He was with a white girl as well. They would hang them all from the highest tree right along with Michelle for being a nigger lover. Back to the situation at hand, what to do? What to do? An idea started to formulate.

"No way I came this far out for nothing. Michelle, tell me every detail about this house, no matter how small. Don't leave anything out," said Spook.

Spook was talking to her again. This was Michelle's chance to get back in good with their family if she could tell them the layout in detail. She put her finger in her mouth and chewed her nails. She looked at the van's ceiling as if the answers were up there. She told Spook everything about the house, right down to the color of the tiles in Marty's Bathroom. They all listened closely. Michelle had a captive audience.

They pulled into a long driveway that led to a house on a hill. The surrounding area was nothing but woods. The house was average size. Some parts looked like they had been added on with makeshift ply boards. It was more like a shack. Rusted out trucks and cars were haphazardly parked all about the landscape. It looked as if some child had been playing with real automobiles and forgot to put his toys away. Tall grass waved in the slight breeze. The place smelled of molded leaves and vegetation. Newer and functional cars and one truck were parked closer to the house.

They pulled up to the house away from the direct sight of the front door. Spook, Isis, and Michelle went inside. Crack Pipe remained in the van with the weapons. Crack Pipe would ease around to the back of the house and bring the guns through the bathroom window after thirty minutes passed. Spook would be in the bathroom. He and Crack Pipe would come out blazing, take their money, drugs, their lives if need be, and be on their way. The plan was crude, but hopefully effective.

***

Stone and Allen had decided they would meet Herbert T at the club. It would be safe enough. They even called in extra security just in case. They also contacted their people on the streets in hopes that someone had seen the Hummer. If they could find the Hummer, chances were they could find Herbert T. Both men had been making calls for close to an hour. Allen had even attempted to reach Spook. Stone made the call to Herbert T. He agreed to meet at Club Establishment.

They were sitting in the club when Dwayne came staggering through the door. His clothes were torn and smudged with dirt and blood. Allen and Stone ran to help him. Dwayne was breathing hard. The bartender saw what was going on and brought some water over to the table.

"Dwayne, what the hell happened to you?" asked Allen.

Dwayne took a big drink of water and immediately spit it out, "Man bring me some hard liquor. This shit will kill you."

The bartender hurried off to get the drink. Dwayne looked at Allen and Stone. "Man they jumped me on my way to work. Three of them came at me from nowhere. I fought the best I could but, as you can see, they overwhelmed me. You can bet all of them felt my presence."

168

Dwayne was a big man. Stone and Allen had seen Dwayne in bar room brawls before and the man could handle himself extremely well.

"What was it all about? I mean did they want from you?" asked Stone.

Dwayne replied, "They asked me shit like who killed Big Mama? Where do you guys live? Where do your girls live? Stuff like that."

Allen and Stone looked at each other. The war had started. "Dwayne, Please tell us you didn't tell them anything," said Allen.

"During our little fight, this police cruiser came down the street. They took off and just left me there on the side walk. The next thing I heard was their tires squealing. Even if they had more time to work me over, I wouldn't have told them anything anyway. Wait until I get my hands on the short and stocky one they called No Neck. He's the one who did this my face.   They didn't get shit form me."

"We need to get you to a hospital," said Allen.

"I'll be okay. My pride is hurt for letting them suckers get the drop on me. I've been busted up worse. I just had to get a hold of you guys and put you up on this bullshit that's in the making. I wasn't even expecting you to be here. I thought I'd have to call all over town to find you," said Dwayne.

"You go get cleaned up. I know you keep a change of clothes in the back. We're meeting Herbert T. here in a matter of minutes," said Stone. He told him about their run in with Herbert T. and No Neck during their trip to Detroit.

"That son of a bitch is coming here!?! I'm gonna fuck him and his boy up. You just leave them to me," Dwayne yelled. He stood up and looked around the club. They didn't have time for this. Someone needed to put a leash on Dwayne.

Stone said, "Dwayne."

But Dwayne didn't hear him. He was enraged.

"Dwayne!" Stone said louder. He had Dwayne's attention. "Allen and I are working things out. This will be a peaceful meeting unless Allen or I say otherwise. Do you understand?"

"Yeah, I understand, but I don't have to like it." Dwayne brushed past them. They watched his massive back as he made his way to the back room.

"I guess it's good to have him on our side," said Allen. It was more a statement than a question.

"Yeah, I wouldn't want him against me," replied Stone.

CHAPTER 18

Stone suddenly jumped to his feet. He punched in numbers on his phone. He walked towards the door. "Come on. Let's go."

"What about our meeting with Herbert T?" said Allen, walking close behind him.

"I think we've been played" said Stone.

They got inside the car. Stone tried to reach Herbert T's phone. "Damn, Herbert T's not answering his phone." His mother's words came to him again. "It's not always a duck. Sometimes it's a duck hunter."

"Stone, what the fuck is you talking about?"

Stone tried calling Tomorrow. "Remember? Dwayne said they were asking him all of those questions. Well one them was where our girls stayed. I almost forgot how this guy thinks. Herbert T kept us busy, so he could gain the upper hand.

"It was a fake meeting. He had no intention on coming. This was a plan. He's getting close to those we care about. He'll have leverage." Stone raced his car through the streets of Battle Creek. "Damn, Tomorrow ain't answering her phone. We must get over there. We've played like a fiddle and beat like a drum."

Allen was deep in thought taking this all in. It made sense. "That's mutha fucka! Stone I swear, if he harmed anyone I'll kill him."

"He knows more about us than I thought. That's the part I'don't understand."

Allen called Carol. Her phone went to voice mail, just like Tomorrow's.

The ride to the girls house was silent. Both men went over it in their heads. How could Herbert T. have moved so fast in a short time? Prayerfully, they were pushing the panic button for nothing. Stone sped through the streets. He ran a few red lights. Allen tried to reach Carol again. When she answered, Allen let out a sigh. He felt better just hearing her voice. Allen told her about Stone's suspicions.

"I was in the shower and left my phone on my bed. Tomorrow is in the shop with some customers," Carol explained.

Allen asked her to check on Tomorrow. Allen and Stone parked in front of the beauty shop. Carol had walked all the way through the house and the shop in search of Tomorrow. She couldn't find her. She went out front door with hopes of seeing Tomorrow and saw Stone and Allen coming towards her.

"She's not in the house or the shop," said Carol. Stone's heart sank. He brushed past her into the shop. Carol and Allen were on his heels.

Stone busted through the door. He looked like a mad man. "Listen up!" he yelled, "Did any of you here see Tomorrow leave?"

The customers shook their heads no along with the employees. Veeda stepped close to the trio, "Two men who pulled up in a nice Hummer came in dressed real good. They paid me fifty dollars to ask Tomorrow to do their hair and nails. She came out to work on them. I didn't see her leave. Is something wrong?"

"We don't know yet. How did these men look?" asked Stone.

Veeda saw their intense looks then said, "Well, let me see. They were both normal sized men. One was light skinned with a beard and a bald head. The other was dark and wore braids with no facial hair. I'm sorry, did I do something wrong?"

"I'll talk to you later," said Carol She put her hand on Veeda's shoulder. Then she turned to Allen and Stone, "We can talk in the house."

She led them through the shop to the house. Tears rolled down her face. She buried her face in Allen's chest. Through her sobs, she managed to say, "Something is wrong, isn't it?"

Neither of the men said anything. Their silence gave her the answer she needed.

"Allen, what are we going to do?"

Stone paced back and forth in the living room.

"Honey, I don't know yet but…" Allen replied.

"But It has to be quick," interrupted Stone. "My baby is at the mercy of a crazed man. I don't care how much money or how many resources I have to use, I must find her. I love her and would never forgive myself if something happens to her."

"What…. What crazed man?" asked Carol.

"We believe it was Herbert T," said Allen. He held both of her hands and looked into her tear filled eyes.

Carol tried pulling herself together so she could help out in any way possible. "We were in the bedroom preparing for our trip when Veeda called. The last words I said to her were I've got you covered. Damn it! I should have went with her."

"Honey, it's not your fault. You can't blame yourself." Allen held her face in his hands.

Stone added, "He's right Carol. If you'd have went with her, then Herbert T would have both of you. Two for one."

"Herbert T! You guys really think that's who has her?" asked Carol. The harsh reality of the situation began to set in.

"Yes, all the signs point to him," said Allen.

"What the fuck was I thinking? How could I let him get to my baby? I've been slipping. Worse yet, I've fell," Stone mumbled to himself.

Allen kissed Carol on her forehead. Then he went over to Stone and placed his hand on his friend's shoulder. Stone had been cussing more lately. Years ago he had dismissed that form of vocabulary. Now he was down on himself. Allen knew all was lost if Stone sank into a state of depression.

"Stone, I need your head right man. This won't bring her back. Come on man. I know you can outthink that mutha fucka. Get your head back on that chess board of life. I know you love her. So does Carol and I do too. Now be at that man I know you can be. We are at war!" barked Allen.

Stone closed his eyes and said a silent prayer. Allen's words hit hard. He was right. His girl was out there somewhere and he was having a pity party. When he opened his eyes they were bloodshot red. He looked like a predator. He was hungry and ready to stalk his prey.

"Carol I apologize. Allen, Thank you. Okay, what to do we know? We know he's down here in a Hummer, and we know he has at least four men with him."

Allen, had never saw his mellow like this, but he felt that Stone was back. To whatever degree, he wasn't certain. "And we know he wants whoever killed his sister."

"We also know that he doesn't like you Stone," added Carol.

Just then, Stone's phone rang. He grabbed it quickly hoping it to be the woman soon to become his wife. The caller I.D. showed not available. Stone answered it. Anxiety could be heard in his voice. "This is Stone!"

He heard a maniacal laugh. Then an excited voice said, "Stoney boy!"

CHAPTER 19

From what Spook could tell, they had no surveillance cameras around the house. A huge, corn fed, hillbilly opened the door. Michelle spoke with a big smile, "Hey Billy Bob. I called ahead. Marty is expecting me and my friends."

Billy Bob spit a long stream of tobacco juice by their feet. "Hold on," he said. He went inside and slammed the door.

His voice could be heard on the porch. "Marty! Michelle's out there and she's got two niggers with her."

Marty yelled, "Let them in, she called earlier."

Billy Bob let them in and closed the door. Billy Bob held a sawed off. 12 gauge shot gun with a modified hand grip. The house smelled of unwashed bodies and meth. Thick crack smoke hung in the air. They followed Billy Bob into a big living room. Three men and two women were sitting down getting high. There was a coffee table, chairs, all kinds of drug paraphernalia, rolling papers, glass pipes, needles, lighters, beers, etc.

One man was sitting on a big bean bag, the two women that were there getting high probably was hot in their day. Now they looked strung out in the worst way, everyone in the room looked up and saw Michelle and her friends.

"Hey Marty," said Michelle to the man sitting on the bean bag.

"Hey Michelle. Billy Bob, check them out," said Marty. He pulled his Tech .9 millimeter out of concealment.

Billy Bob did as he was told. In the process of checking them, he gripped Spook's nut sack a little to hard. Spook fought back the urge to break his jaw. His hands roamed even longer over Isis and Michelle's breasts and ass cheeks.

"They're clean Marty. Except Michelle had this knife in her pants." Billy Bob held the knife up with two fingers letting it swing back and forth for Marty to see.

How Michelle could be that stupid? She might get them all killed. Michelle should have won an Oscar for her performance.

"Marty, remember? You gave me that knife the last time I was out here to cut my dope.," said Michelle.

"She is right. Give it back to her," demanded Marty.

Michelle walked over to Billy Bob and snatched the knife back.

"Sorry about that, but you can never be too safe," said Marty. He placed his Tech nine back below the table. Then he looked at the others. "Y'all can go to the other room. Give these people y'all seats. Can't you see we got business? Take y'all shit with y'all. When you need more you know where I'm at." He cut his eyes at the small group at the table.

178

They left the room reluctantly, with the exception of Billy Bob. He stood by the door against the wall with his arms crossed. Billy Bob looked like he got off inflicting pain on others. The sawed off rested in the crook of his arm.

Spook, Michelle, and Isis took the chairs at the coffee table. Michelle sat closest to Marty. Marty looked at Spook, "How much do you want to spend big fella?"

"I'll spend a hundred on meth for now. If it's top shelf shit, then I may be willing to spend a few grand later. Michelle told me that you don't mind if we get high here," said Spook. He noticed the rebel flag on the wall.

"Yeah that's cool. Just make sure that the house man gets his cut. That's me by the way," Marty said. He displayed his tobacco stained teeth in a smile. Marty was small framed with stringy blond hair down to his shoulders. It was plain to see that his life style was stripping him of his weight and health. His face was sunken in and darkness surrounded both of his eye sockets. He was so skinny. It was as if his skin was stretched over his face. He was like a skeleton. Spook tore a hundred dollar bill from his stack.

Greed filled Marty's eyes. "Billy Bob, get the stuff and sit yo ass down somewhere. You make my clients nervous."

Billy Bob had red hair and a red beard. He wore overalls with no shirt and he had hair all over his body. He reminded Spook of the silver backed ape, only with red hair. Billy Bob left the room and came back with a black garbage bag He handed it to Marty. Then he posted back at his door. Marty opened a small panel on the bottom of the

179

coffee table, pulled out some triple beam scales, reached in the black plastic bag, and brought out a few small white bricks. Spook and the girls watched as he weighed out portions of the meth.

Marty gave Spook a hundred dollars worth. A female came in the room. Spook hadn't seen her before. She wasn't there when he first came in. She wore Daisy Dukes that were cut into her little ass. She also wore a sports bra and was barefooted. She was skinny as a rail. She came and sat on the other side of Marty. Spook guessed she was Marty's girlfriend. Billy Bob got a chair and sat on the other side of Spook. His shot gun was on the floor where he could reach it. He was farthest from Spook.

"Hi Michelle," said the skinny woman.

"Hey Crystal. Girl are you okay?" asked Michelle.

Michelle and Isis looked at Crystal with distaste. She looked horrific. You could see the filth under her fingernails. She scratched and picked at herself. Meth Monster Spook thought. Michelle and Isis wondered if they had looked that bad before Spook cleaned them up.

"Hell naw I ain't okay. Marty's out here doing his thing and I'm back there having to get myself off. I'm sexually frustrated," said Crystal. She slapped Marty on his back. It made him cough from the smoke he had just taken in from his pipe.

Spook and the girls put meth on their pipes. They acted like nothing else mattered except getting high.

"What in tar nation did you go do that for you stupid as heifer? You almost made me spill my shit on the floor. You just wait until our company leaves. I'm gone give you some of this white dick. Just be patient!" yelled Marty.

Billy Bob smiled for the first time. Those two went at it all the time and it was funny to him.

Crystal said, "Well if I can't get no dick then you give me some more of your dope."

Spook gave Marty, the house man, a nice portion of the dope that he just bought.

Marty took it and split it in half. Half of it went to Crystal and half to Billy Bob, who immediately went to getting high. It made him relax more. Crystal sat by Marty on the bean bag. The dope made vacuum cleaner sounds as she sucked it through her pipe.

"Crystal you need to slow down. You've been smoking like a choo-choo train," Marty said. She kept smoking and ignored him. "So what do you think, uh, what is your name anyway?" Marty directed his question to Spook.

"I go by Spook."

Marty snickered at the name. Billy Bob busted out laughing. They couldn't control themselves. They laughed out loud and hearty. Everyone, even Crystal was surprised by the laughter.

Spook looked back and forth at the two men. He wondered what was wrong with them. "What so damn funny?" asked Spook.

The men's laughter subsided. Marty said, "My forefathers were calling your kind Spook's since before I was born. Now here you come with the name and proud of it. I guess that's just like your kind used to hate the word NIGGER. Now we don't have to call y'all that. You do it yourselves. You even sing about it in your songs. Oh sure, you guys say nigga instead of NIGGER. You guys say it with an A but it still means the same thing."

Spook was burning mad but held himself in check and tired not to show it. It was painfully obvious that Marty was racist. Although he was right about the word nigger being widely used by blacks when some so many had fought and died for civil rights. At least Marty was open about his prejudices, not like many who hid it. So, in that small degree, Spook had respect for him.

Marty continued, "It's rare that niggers come this far back in the woods. Boy don't you go getting uppity and angry. We're just poking fun at you."

The room went silent. Marty broke the silence by saying, "Damn, all this laughing has given me a headache." He reached in the coffee table and brought out a small bottle and handed the bottle to Spook.

Spook was still pissed. "What the fuck you want me to do with this?"

Michelle and Isis were getting high but watchful of what was going around them. Billy Bob and Crystal had their eyes on Spook. Spook removed the cap from the bottle. Then he tried giving the bottle back to Marty.

"I have the damnedest time getting to the asprin. Can you take that cotton out first?" asked Marty.

Spook took the cotton out and handed Marty the aspirin bottle. Marty took the bottle of aspirin with a big ass shit eating grin on his face. Spook realized his mistake. The joke was on him.

Marty couldn't wait to say, "My Grandpappy told me that niggers was a good at picking cotton."

Marty and Billy Bob roared with laughter. Billy Bob slapped his knee. It took all of Spook's strength not to just start punching. He didn't care who, just so he punched somebody. The joke was on him for the moment. He would absorb the humility and bite his tongue until the time was right. He stole a look at his watch. Five more minutes. Crack Pipe don't fail me now, he thought.

"I'm sitting here trying to get high. There is no cause for you to insult me and my race!" yelled Spook. He was ready to spring for Marty's throat.

"Whoa, whoa, whoa, there big fella. Like I said, I'm just funning," Marty said still halfway laughing.

"Marty, I brought him here so we could get high and you could make some money. What's the hell wrong with you?" asked Michelle not liking the sudden turn of events.

"Bitch, I don't give a fuck about you and your nigger loving ass anyway. I don't cotton to our pure blood white women mixing with niggers no how," growled Marty.

"Yeah Michelle, you done went and got yo self some jungle fever?" asked Crystal.

"Fuck you, stank hoe. You skinny ass meth monster," retorted Michelle.

Crystal gave Michelle the middle finger. She said, "Fuck you. Nigger lover."

"Bitch ass. Crystal, you fuck with Michelle, you fucking with me. Don't get fucked up in this motha fucka," said Isis.

"Bitch, you in my man's house. You can get your mix blooded ass the fuck out,"

said Crystal, cowering behind Marty.

Isis said, "I'll leave, but not before I knick your stanking white ass."

"Marty get rid of them, I'm ready for you to fuck me," whined Crystal.

"Bitch, that's why yo ass is tripping, cause won't nobody give yo nasty ass no dick? Crystal you can just shut the fuck up. You can't make nobody leave. Look at you, you once a month bleeding, cum burping bitch!" said Michelle, with fire in her eyes.

"Shut up, all of you! I run this mother fucking show!" yelled Marty.

"You want me to put them out Marty?" asked Billy Bob.

"No, not so fast," said Marty, then pointed to Spook, "I want the rest of his money."

Spook looked Marty in the eyes. Spook knew that look too well. He stood up fast. Billy Bob stood with him. He put the sawed off to the back of Spook's neck. "How do you homeboy's say it in the hood? Stick up Bitch!" Tobacco and spit spilled from his mouth as he coked the sawed off.

CHAPTER 20

It was Herbert T. He was the only one who called him Stoney Boy. Stone wasted no time getting straight to the point. "So you weren't sincere after all. The visit to the pool hall, the fake meeting and beating my bar manager. But why take my fiancé?" asked Stone.

Herbert T answered, "Listen Stoney Boy, you know I'm in it to win it, I've always told you that. As for your future wife, I don't know what you're talking about. I don't like talking much on phones. You never know who might be listening. I can say the last time I saw her she was crying and missing you."

Stone knew Herbert T had Tomorrow. He had just said it in so many words. Stone also knew he wouldn't openly admit to having her on the phone. He was covering his ass in case the police were listening. Herbert T. was a slick one. Stone would seek his own justice.

"You son-of- ah-bitch! If you harm her, I'll fuck your wanna be ass up and who's ever with you," shouted Stone.

"Stoney Boy, temper, temper. What happened to the gentlemen in you? Your mouth is dirty and should be washed out with soap. Do you kiss your mother with that mouth?"

" I meant what I said Herbert T. If you…"

Herbert T. interrupted, "Nigga, you ain't in no position to demand shit. Listen closely because I won't repeat myself.

We'll meet at your club tomorrow. Don't try no nickel slick shit Stoney or people we love may have accidents."

The line went dead. Herbert T had hung up. Stone knew exactly what he meant. Herbert T. had implied if Stone tried anything, Tomorrow would get hurt. Stone made Carol and Allen aware of the new developments. He called to check on his mother. She had arrived at her destination safely. Stone told her to stay put until he took care of some business. He would check back in once it was done. They said their I love you's and she told him to be careful.

Everyone agreed that calling in the police would be like signing Tomorrow's death warrant. Stone and Allen dropped Carol off at the hotel room. Allen told her to keep the phone line open. After making sure Carol was secure, they drove back to their club in silence. Allen felt so helpless. He could see that his good and trusted friend was seriously distraught and angry. All because of his brother.

Somehow Allen felt responsible. If he hadn't brought Spook into the fold, these people's lives would be running smoothly. Allen's mind was occupied with how he could fix things. The answers seemed to evade him.

Stone had made his mind up to save his love at all cost. Whoever got in his way, woe to them. Even if he got her back, he wanted death to befall Herbert T. His vengeance on him would be more than an emotional response. It would be punishment for all of his wrongs, old and new. The old saying came to mind; When you go for vengeance, dig two graves. At this point death was welcomed. Herbert T. had even went after his mother. Stone was at the point he didn't care about dying. He would take Herbert T. out with him, just so he could make Tomorrow safe.

The meeting with Herbert T. wouldn't be until the following day, so they both had a drink and filled Dwayne in on the latest. They both left deciding that nothing could be done at this point. Allen went to the room with Carol. She had worried herself sick. They just held each other the whole night.

Stone went home. Sleep didn't come easy to Stone. He tossed and turned. He went over in his head how things had went so wrong. He needed to focus his efforts on how to rectify things.

The following day Allen and Stone hooked up at the club. Dwayne was there. You could see the black eye and bruises from his encounter with Herbert T's minions. Dwayne saw them enter. He grabbed a bottle of Cognac and went to join them in the back. "So that mutha fucka's really coming here?" asked Dwayne.

"Yeah, if he's true to his word. He should be here within the hour," replied Allen.

"I just want Tomorrow back. This whole thing has got me so messed up inside. Herbert T. is holding all the cards," said Stone.

Allen announced, "Stone I want you to give up Spook."

"You what?" said Stone. He was surprised.

"You heard me. When Herbert T. comes here, you tell him all you know about Spook. I've thought long and hard about this. If it wasn't for him, none of this would be happening. Besides, Spook can handle himself. Now do what I asked you."

"But Allen, that will make him come after you in hopes of drawing Spook out from wherever he is."

Dwayne just looked back and forth between the two, listening to whatever plan they came up with.

"Stone, I'm at the point where I don't care if he comes after me. We're going to get Tomorrow back. You and I are in this together. We ride or die."

Stone really admired his trusted friend. They stood, shook hands, and embraced. Stone's phone rang. He knew it was Herbert T. "Hello."

Allen and Dwayne watched as Stone's facial expressions changed. "Okay Dorothy, slow down, is everyone alright?" Stone said into his phone. They could hear Dorothy's voice coming from Stone's phone. "Allen will be there soon." Stone hung up the phone.

"Stone, what's going on? And what did you just volunteer me for when you know we have a meeting."

"That was Dorothy. Herbert T's boys just roughed up a couple of the girls. Dorothy was beat the worst but said she cut one of them good. For some unknown reason, security was pulled from that building. No one's there now but the girls and the operation is shut down until we can get to the bottom of this."

"Hell naw! Are you crazy Stone? I'm not leaving you to deal with that twisted ass mutha fucka by yourself. He probably wants to split us."

"Allen, Herbert T has stayed one step ahead of us. He is hurting the people that we care about, not to mention slowing down our cash flow. When Herbert T gets here. I'm going to mention Spook's name. It is my wish for you not to be here. You go check on Dorothy and the girls. Dwayne will be here with me. He'll watch my back."

Stone saw that Allen was going to protest. He stopped him before he said anything by holding up his hand. "Allen, please just go before he gets here. Please mellow. Do this for me."

"Stone's right. He won't be by himself. I'll be here and I'll have his back. I have interest in dealing out some pain, if the situation calls for it," Dwayne interjected.

"I don't know. I don't like it. It's a shitty plan," Allen commented.

"Go Allen. I can probably make this work better without you being here. Spook being your brother just may anger him more and Tomorrow might get hurt. So go on, get out of here. Time is ticking," explained Stone.

Allen was totally against this plan. It was way too risky, but he wanted Tomorrow back as bad as Stone. All this was his brother's doing, so Allen decided he would respect

Stone's wishes and leave. Allen pointed his finger at Dwayne and said, "You be on top of your game. Don't let anything happen to my mellow." He downed his drink and looked Stone in his eyes, "And you be safe." Allen walked out the door.

Stone looked at his watch. "He should be here shortly," he said to Dwayne.

They walked to the front of the club. "Is there anything I should know or do when he gets here?" asked Dwayne.

"It's just me and you. We don't do anything unless we have to. You got that?"

"Yeah, I got it."

Fifteen minutes later in walked Herbert T. and No Neck Norman. They took seats across from Stone and Dwayne.

Stone looked at Herbert T with contempt. "I never knew you would stoop so low. Where's Tomorrow?"

"That's the difference between you and me. I've got the patience to see things through," replied Herbert T.

Stone's eyes bored a hole through Herbert T's head. "I said, where is Tomorrow?"

"She's fine. Don't worry about her. You should be more concerned about yourself. Say, where is that guy that you're always with? And who is this mutha fucka anyway?" said Herbert T. pointing to Dwayne.

"You know who the fuck I am. You had your boys do a number on me and this is one of them right here!" Dwayne pointed his thick finger at No Neck.

"That was just our way of getting some attention. Don't take it so personal, tough guy," said No Neck with a smile.

"Damn all this finger pointing. Let's get down to business. Who killed my sister?" asked Herbert T.

"First, I need to know if you have her and if she's alright," demanded Stone.

Herbert T. nodded his head towards No Neck who took out an envelope from his suit pocket and slid it across the table to Stone.

"Can a guy get something to drink in this joint?" asked Herbert T. He hunched his shoulders and lit his thick cigar.

Stone nodded his head towards Dwayne to get them something to drink. Dwayne left for the bar to bring back a bottle. Stone looked down at the envelope half scared to open it. He picked it up and slowly opened it. Herbert T and No Neck looked on with amusement. They were like parents watching their child open a Christmas present.

The contents of the envelope were Tomorrow's earrings. Stone had bought them for her a long time ago. His blood boiled. There were some hair shavings and a big red toe nail in the envelope too. It was definitely from a female's foot and blood was attached to the end of it.

"Those are her pubic hairs. No Neck pulled her big toe nail out with pliers. Man you should have heard that bitch scream," bragged Herbert T.

Stone threw a punch at No Neck's face. No Neck tried to block the punch, but it was too late. Stone was much quicker. The blow was solid. It knocked No Neck from his chair. Herbert T grabbed for his gun.

Stone stood up and pulled both of his .357 magnums. One was at Herbert T's forehead and the other aimed at No Neck Norman. Herbert T gave up his attempts to get his gun and raised both hands high in the air. No Neck froze mid–motion when Stone cocked the hammer.

"Stay down No Neck. Tomorrow is the only reason I don't kill both of you. Dwayne, get over here."

Stone hit Herbert T. upside his head with one of his guns. Herbert T. let out a moan. Blood trickled down from his head.

"I'm gonna make you suffer real slow for that Stone. You'll beg me to kill you," barked Herbert T.

"Last time Herb, where is Tomorrow?"

"If you kill me, my boys will kill her."

Dwayne had made his way over with a sawed off and stood by Stone. He aimed his gun at No Neck. Since Dwayne had him covered, Stone now pointed both of his guns at Herbert T's head.

"I won't ask," was all Stone had a chance to say. He felt a hard blow the back of his head. He fell in what seemed to be slow motion. He tried to stop himself but the gravitational pull was too strong. It was as if the floor was pulling his face to it. He hit the floor hard. A sea of darkness overcame him.

Stone woke up a few minutes later. His head was banging with pain. He was still on the barroom floor. Herbert T., No Neck, and Dwayne were standing above him. He was barely conscious. Stone's eyes adjusted. Where were his guns? The answer presented itself. No Neck had them pointed at his face. The deadly weapons looked very menacing. Dwayne had his arm around Herbert T. What the fuck was going on?

"I know you never saw this coming," said Dwayne.

What did he mean? Was this some type of bad dream? He was being betrayed by the man who they trusted. God, please let this be a dream, he thought to himself. His brain processed the grim reality of the situation. It was information overload and his head was still ached from the blow.

"Herbert T. and I have been hustling together since high school. We had plans to take over your operation even before Big Mama got killed. All the time you and Allen thought I was working for you. I was really working with Herbert T. to bring the both of you down.

"I had No Neck beat me up so you guys would believe me. It was me who gave all the useful information to Herbert T,

194

and yes, it was me who just busted you upside your head," Dwayne confessed.

"I know that Spook killed my sister and that Allen is his younger brother. They will both get theirs. We had to bring you down first. You appear to be the smart one of the bunch," said Herbert T.

Tears rolled down Stone's face.

Dewayne was enjoying this. He said, "It was me who set up you bitch. She's in bad shape Stone. You should see her."

Stone's mother's words echoed in his head again. "If it looks like a duck, and quacks like a duck, It's a duck hunter."

Herbert T. chimed in, "Hey Stoney boy you don't look so good. I hope Dwayne here didn't give you a concussion with that gun upside your head. I want you aware of me destroying you from the inside out."

Stone had made a major slip up with Dwayne. This man had unlimited access to their entire operation. It didn't take a genius to figure out that it was Dwayne who pulled the security off of Dorothy's building. He knew these men would kill him. Right now he didn't care. He just wanted to get his hands around Dwayne's or Herbert T's throat. It didn't matter which one. Either of them would do. Stone collected all the strength he could. He tried to lift himself from the floor to lunge at the men, only to find the heel of No Neck's shoe meeting the side of his face. Stone laid there on the cold floor unconscious as blood flowed from his mouth.

CHAPTER 21

Spook had a double barrel shot gun hard against his neck. He couldn't believe it. Spook gave a quick thought to how Ironic things had turned out to be. He was there to stickup the white boys and now the script had flipped. He had become a victim of his own game. The old street saying was true, the same thing that makes you laugh will make you cry.

Isis and Michelle wanted to run to the rest room. They hoped Crack Pipe was in there with the guns, at the very least placed them in there, or something. Just when they thought things couldn't get any worse, the two couples in the back room came to the door telling Marty that they would be back later because his house had gotten too noisy since those uppity blacks arrived. They saw Billy Bob with the gun to Spook's neck and thought nothing of it. Marty told them come back in a couple of hours and the niggers would be gone for good. Three of them headed out the door while the fourth told Marty that she would be using his rest room on the way out. Marty told her to go ahead and if she heard some niggers screaming not to pay it any attention. She smiled at the thought and told them to have fun.

Marty turned to Spook, See what you done went and did? You done run off good respectable white folk."

Michelle reached in her purse trying to feel for her knife. Marty pointed his finger at Spook.

"I want you to take all the money out of your pockets. Then we'll go out to your vehicle and see what we can muster up out of there." Spook laid wads of money on the coffee table very slowly. He did not want Billy Bob to think that he was trying something and pull the trigger. What the fuck happened to Crack Pipe?

Spook's mind raced with thoughts of how to get out of this. Michelle had her hand on the knife. She gave Isis a look that she was going for it. Crystal was enjoying it all. She was still getting high and rubbing on Marty's dick. Crystal noticed him getting hard through his pants. She hadn't been able to get him hard like this for days. She figured that excitement was enhancing his sexual arousal.

"Hey Michelle, you nigger loving Bitch, I bet you hate you got mixed up with these spear chuckers now, huh?" said Crystal hoping to turn Marty on even more.

Just then, they heard a woman scream. It was followed by the sound of someone running fast in their direction. Marty was on his feet aiming his Tech Nine in the general direction of the footsteps. The woman came into view. Her shirt was on but her pants and panties were down around one leg while her other leg was free. Apparently she had been using the rest room and got up off the toilet in a hurry. The bottom half of her body was exposed with urine dripping from between her legs.

She said, "Marty, I was sitting on your toilet when some damn nigger came in through your bathroom window."

"What the fuck?" said Marty.

No sooner then he said that, Crack Pipe materialized strapped with two guns in the waist of his pants and two in his hands. Spook and the girls smiled. Crack Pipe never looked so good. He let loose with both guns. He fired wildly in Marty's direction. Marty and Billy Bob were confused.

Billy Bob went to aim at Crack Pipe. Spook was ready. He took advantage of the distraction and grabbed for the sawed off. Both of the big men wrestled for possession of the shot gun. The next events happened in a matter of seconds.

Marty didn't have time to aim his gun at this new threat. He did the next best thing. He dropped his gun and with the same motion he grabbed the girl from the rest room. Marty held her in front of him as a human shield. Crack Pipe squeezed off shot after shot. The woman's body jerked as hot lead tore into her. The force drove Marty backwards. She continued her blood curdling scream until bullets took her very last breath.

Marty's gun fell right by Crystal. She grabbed for the gun. Isis saw her and dived over the table. She crashed into Crystal head first.

The three that went outside heard the blood curdling scream and gun shots. They rushed back into the see what's going on. Crack Pipe heard them approach behind him. He turned and fired non-stop. The walls and the three who ran into the house were riddled with bullets. They died with hot lead in their faces, necks and bodies. Blood splattered the walls. Cries and gunshots rang out through the house.

Crack Pipe had his back to Marty as he sprayed gunfire. Marty saw his chance. He let the woman's lifeless body fall and jumped out the picture window. The curtains shielded him from most of the sharp glass, however, some shards of glass stuck him as he hit the ground. This caused him much pain.

Spook continued to wrestle with Billy Bob. The big white man proved to be very strong. He maneuvered Spook to where Spook's back was on the seat of the chair. Billy Bob stood over him with the shotgun barrel on his neck trying to choke him. All that Spook could do was hold the barrel of the gun with both of his hands and try to stop Billy Bob from crushing his windpipe. Both men were grunting and using all of their strength. Then Michelle came up behind Billy Bob. She had both of her fist balled up together and began to hit Billy Bob in his back, over and over again.

Spook thought to himself that she had heart, but this bitch gotta know that her tiny fist to this big motha fucka's back ain't gonna do nothing. She continued hiting him repeatedly. Billy Bob's hold on the gun started to weaken. Michelle didn't stop hitting him in his back. Billy Bob let out a groan of intense pain and let go of the gun. He turned around to confront his attacker. He back handed Michelle. She yelped like a wounded animal. His mighty blow caused her to sail across the room into the wall. The air was knocked from her when she came in contact with the hard surface. Spook thought Michelle was just hitting Billy Bob in the back. She had been stabbing him. The knife protruded from his back. There was a fast growing big red spot forming. It was blood.

Michelle was no longer a threat. Billy Bob turned back to face Spook and found himself looking down the barrel of his own .12 gauge sawed off. Spook smiled and fired both barrels. Billy Bob was peppered with buck shot. The shot took his whole head off. His body fell not too far from Isis and Crystal. They were still rolling and fighting on the floor. Spook wasted no time in taking control of the situation.

"Crack Pipe! Marty went out the window. Go get him!" shouted Spook.

Crack Pipe laid three of the guns on the table and some ammunition too. Then he headed out the door in search of Marty. Spook took a quick inventory of his surroundings. Everything seemed to be going his way. He made sure the guns were loaded.

Isis was on top of Crystal, holding her skinny arms. Michelle stood and shook her head trying to regain her balance. Spook saw that her hands were bloody along with her face and shirt.

"You okay?" he asked.

She replied, "Yeah I'm fine. This is Billy Bob's blood."

"What do you want me to do with her baby?" asked Isis. She didn't take her eyes off Crystal.

"Beat that bitch's ass," Spook growled.

Isis yelled in her ear, "Bitch I'm going to beat you ugly!"

Isis began to pummel Crystal's face. No matter how hard Crystal tried to stop the blows, Isis' fist got through. Isis bloodied her nose and knocked some teeth down her throat. Crystal started to choke. Spook figured that was enough and Crystal should be softened up enough to talk. He told Isis to stop. Isis was breathing hard and still on top of Crystal.

Spook handed Michelle a gun from the table. "Go help Crack Pipe find Marty."

Michelle went out the door. Spook walked over to Isis, "Let that bitch up. Take all that money and dope out of the table. Here take your gun baby."

Isis got off Crystal, got her gun from Spook, then did what Spook asked.

Crystal tried to dislodge the teeth that Isis had knocked down her throat by coughing. Her face was a bloody mess. She managed to get up on her hands and knees and spit a couple of teeth out. She swallowed the rest. She continued to cough and take in deep breaths.

Now that her pathway was cleared, she began to breathe normal again. What light Crystal could see through her swollen eyes was overshadowed by someone standing in front of her. Her eyes followed the legs up the body and then to Spook's face. He had his Desert Eagle in his hand.

"Yeah bitch, the worm has turned. You get to live your life if you answer my questions. So where you think yo boy Marty ran off to? Is there any house that he can go to nearby?" asked Spook.

Crystal didn't say a word. She just looked at Spook with hate filled eyes. Then she spit a glob of blood on his pants. She jumped up screaming and clawing at Spook's eyes. A red hole appeared right between Crystal's eyes. She back paddled until she was stopped by the wall. She slid down slowly until her body came to rest on the floor with her legs twisted below her. She was dead. Spook turned to see Isis in a police stance. Both of her hands were holding the gun and smoke was escaping from the barrel. It was just like on TV.

Isis knew the disapproving look that Spook had was for her. "Sorry baby, but don't no bitch come at my man like that."

Spook said, "Damn Isis. I wanted to find out where Marty ran off to before you killed her."

"I think I know where he might have went."

"Where?"

"Remember Michelle said he had a lab around back? Well I figured that someone who loves meth the way he does wouldn't leave all that stuff even if the world was being invaded by aliens."

Isis made a good point. She and Michelle had become seasoned to the hard game. Isis handed Spook the shoe box filled with money and the sack of dope.

"Okay, let's go find the others," said Spook.

They stepped over the bloody bodies. Spook was grateful that Crack Pipe had came through after all. They walked from the house carefully. They placed the money and dope in the van. Spook and Isis went around to the back of the house. They saw Michelle and Crack Pipe coming from a beat up barn.

"We looked around the outside of the house first. Then we just peeped in there." Michelle nodded towards the barn. "I was telling Crack Pipe how we need to be real careful around meth making chemicals. They're highly flammable and highly explosive."

"What's in there?" asked Spook

"We can't find Marty. There's all kind of shit in there. Buckets of stuff with tubes running everywhere," added Crack Pipe

Spook headed in to look for himself, with the others trailing behind. He stopped. "Y'all heard what Michelle said about this stuff being unstable. Be very careful."

This barn looked like what you see in a mad scientist movie. The chemical smell was strong. All of them held their noses.

Spook said, "I'm wondering how we can take some of this stuff with us. We got what we came for. However, Marty is still out there somewhere and that is my biggest concern at this point. Be mindful that a man is around here somewhere and he wants us dead. Hurry up and search. We must get out of here."

Spook started looking through stuff, picking up boxes, bottles, and packages. Then he ran across a suitcase of some sort. Spook went to open it and knocked it off the table. It hit the floor and money spilled from it in stacks. It was the mother load. Spook told them to hurry and help him put the money back in the suitcase.

A blinking light caught his attention under the table. Upon closer examination, Spook saw a timer attached to the underside of the table. The timer was connected to plastic explosives. Somehow they must have activated it. The time displayed twenty seconds.....19...18....17....16.... Michelle, Isis, and Crack Pipe were still grabbing bundles of money. Spook grabbed the case, slammed it shut, and said loud as he could, "Leave it! Run for your lives!"

They knew not to question Spook, especially when he gave them his back moving at a high speed. Spook was the first one out of the barn with the case of money in his hand. Isis was on his heels. Michelle was close behind Isis, but Crack Pipe lagged too far behind. He had grabbed the rest of the money on the barn floor. His hands were full as he ran dropping money with each step. Spook, Isis, and Michelle had made it to where they guessed to be a safe distance away. Crack Pipe might not make it clear of the blast zone. Spook, Isis, and Michelle cheered him on, motioning with their hands to hurry.

Crack Pipe tripped over a rock. This probably saved his life. The explosion was deafening. Debris flew over Crack Pipe's body. Spook Isis, and Michelle were blown to the ground. They felt the heat on their faces from the blast. Along with the loud boom came a white flash. What was once a barn was now a pile of rubble up in flames. Debris was scattered everywhere. Pieces fell from the sky. The house went up in flames as well.

The three got to their feet. "Damn!" they said at the same time.

They heard coughing. It was Crack Pipe. He was covered with dirt and debris. As he stood, he dusted himself off. "Okay everybody, let's get in the van and put some distance from this place."

Spook said, "I wanted Marty. but no telling who heard that explosion or who can see those flames and smoke."

Crack Pipe went to the driver's side. When Crack Pipe opened the door a foot kicked him in his face. Crack Pipe never saw it coming. He hit the ground hard. Marty sat in the driver's seat. His face had been sliced pretty bad from jumping through the window. Blood was still streaming down his face. In one hand he held an A.R.15 assault rifle. He pointed it in their direction. In his other hand was a block of C4.

Spook cursed himself for not being more alert. He gave Marty props because this is what he would have done if the situation was reversed.

"You!" he yelled.

Marty said, "Yeah it's me, you stupid spear chucker nigger. I see you and your whores tripped my anti-theft, anti Police, booby trap device. I got to give it to you. That was pretty clever having your boy come through my bathroom window like that. The only reason you're still alive is because I want my $100,000 back and then some. So, you're going to take me to your stash."

"And why would I some stupid shit like that?" asked Spook.

"Because I'm the one with nothing to lose and in case you didn't notice, I'm the one with the gun and the C4, fucking Idiot." Then Marty held up the C4 so they could get a good look at it. "All I have to do is push this red button on this device here and you and your friends can cancel Christmas. I have no love for your kind. I would like nothing more than to take some of you with me to that great big meth lab in the sky. Now all of you get in and take me to your place. Pretty soon this whole place will be crawling with pigs and we know how you spades feel about pork. Now get in!"

Marty was right about the police. Spook had no doubt Marty would kill them all. So he told the girls to get in. Michelle got into the passenger seat and Isis and Spook got in through the sliding door.

Marty kept his gun trained on them and asked, "Which one of you will be driving since he won't?"

Crack Pipe had been beat and kicked around all of his adult life by dope dealers. Compared to them Marty kicked like an old lady. He faked being unconscious. The driver's door was still open. Crack Pipe aimed his gun from where he lay on the ground at the back of Marty's head and pulled the trigger.

His gun made aloud a click. It was empty but the sound was enough to make Marty take his eyes off Spook and the girls. That was all Spook needed. He couldn't stand straight up in the van. He hunched over bending his leg and rushed Marty like a bull seeing red. Marty felt someone bump into him. The block of C- fell out of his hands. Spook tried to take the gun. The assault rifle was set on automatic. It went off shooting holes in the van's ceiling. Everything went in slow motion. Spook and Marty stopped tugging back and forth with the assault rifle. The girls gasped. All four of them watched as the C4 came nearer to hitting the floor of the van. After a lifetime, the C4 landed and bounced. It came to rest under the passenger seat. There wasn't a person in the van who didn't give silent thanks. Spook and Marty resumed tussling within the confined space of the van.

"Fuck this!" said Michelle. She maneuvered herself close to the men. She placed her gun to Marty's temple and squeezed the trigger. Marty's body fell out of the van onto Crack Pipe.

He pushed Marty's bloody body off him and commenced to beating Marty in what remained of his face with the butt of his gun.

Spook looked at Michelle. Michelle went to the back of the van and gave Isis a fist bump. She had developed into a cold blooded bitch right along with Isis. Spook yelled out the window at Crack Pipe. "Man he's dead, let's get the hell out of here!" Crack Pipe looked up at Spook with empty eyes.

"Damn, ya'll mutha fuckas really need some dope bad. Michelle get us the hell out of here. Crack Pipe, you go back there with Isis and get something into your system. You done well."

Spook examined the block of plastic explosives. It had a red button for immediate detonation and a small digital clock for a timer. Spook started to toss it out the window but thought better of it. He saw what this stuff could do and had plenty of respect for its awesome power. It might come in handy some other time. He put it in a small box and placed the box under the seat for the time being. Crack Pipe was feeling much better after smoking a little crack to calm his nerves.

Once they were off the dirt road, Michelle pulled over and now Crack Pipe was back behind the wheel driving. They had a good ways to go before getting back to Battle Creek. Michelle gave Crack Pipe directions on how to navigate through small rural towns. They drove a different route back from which they had come. The van it had blood on the seats and bullets holes in the roof. Spook realized that he would have to burn this van and buy another one.

"Thank you Crack Pipe. You really came through back there," said Michelle.

"Yeah bro, I didn't know you had it in you," added Isis.

Spook said, "All of you come through with flying colors. We can kick back for a while now. After we rest for a few days, I'm taking y'all to Detroit. From there we will travel the States. I'm going to put together a business where we won't have to work so hard. We'll work smarter, not harder and we'll be taking less risks. Y'all are alright in my book.

I told y'all, just follow my simple rules and we'll go to the top. Just do what I tell you and be patient. It gets greater later. Now let's go get cleaned up and rested up."

Spook gazed out the window at the beautiful homes they had out here. They were spaced far apart. Some were about a mile apart with privacy fences. Then he saw a sweet S.U.V in a driveway. This was the first Hummer he'd seen since getting out of prison. He remembered seeing them on T.V. and in magazines, but never in person. There couldn't have been many of them around due to the heavy price tag. Whoever owned it had money. Spook didn't like the color though. It was powder blue.

CHAPTER 22

Allen checked on Carol. She was okay and all of her basic needs were met. Knowing that she was in a safe place and out of harm's way allowed him to think more clearly. He felt guilty about leaving Stone to fend for himself. After convincing Carol to stay put, he drove back to the club. The inside lights weren't on anymore, but Stone's car was still there. Dwayne's truck had been parked out front earlier, but now it wasn't. Allen unlocked the door to the club and went in ever so cautiously. He didn't see anyone.

No one was in the office either. It was strange. He saw some glasses on the table in the VIP section. Two more than when Allen had sat there earlier. There was some liquor left in them. A stubbed out cigar was in the ashtray. Neither Stone or Dwayne smoked cigars. Herbert T. had been there.

He saw something wet on the floor. He rubbed the toe of his shoe across the red stain. It was half dried blood. Whose blood was it? Things were getting stranger by the minute. Allen tried reaching Stone on his cell phone. He had a feeling it was a waste of time. He got Stone's answering service. He tried Stone's home phone and got the same. Where could he be? Allen didn't know what was going on but somehow he knew he should leave this club. He couldn't shake the feeling that it was no longer safe. He went to his car. As he put the car in drive, his phone rang.

Allen answered, "Yeah!"

It was Spook. "Hey lil brother, I see you been blowing my phone up. What's the deal-e-o?"

"Spook, where the hell are you? Things have went from sugar to shit out here."

"I'm with my girls at a hotel. You want to come over here and get your knob polished?"

"Damn them bucket heads Spook. This is life or death out here man. I really need to speak with you. Some shit went down in a major way."

Spook could tell by his brother's voice that it was serious. He and Allen weren't on good terms at the present time, but he would kill anyone who messed with his baby brother. "Okay listen, write this address down. Meet me in twenty minutes. Does that work for you?"

"Yeah, that works? Where are you?"

Spook gave him the address and room number. Allen hung up and called his home phone to check for messages. No one had called. He tried calling Stone again. He still wasn't answering. He hit his fist on the steering wheel out of anger and frustration. "Damn! Stone, where the hell are you!" He shouted out loud.

His phone rang again. It was Carol. He took a deep breath and calmed himself before he answered, "Hello baby. You lonely there at that hotel room by yourself?"

Carol replied, "Allen, I'm always lonely without you. When will you be back?"

"Right now I can't say Carol. Stone is nowhere to be found. He's not answering his phone. His car is still at the club. Dwayne is missing too. I found someone's blood on the floor in the VIP section at the club."

"You don't think he's in any trouble do you?"

"I'm not sure what to think. Problems are piling up and I don't have any solutions. Any word on Tomorrow?"

"No, I keep trying her cell phone and the house. I can't help but feel that there's something more I can do other than polish this seat with my ass. I'm worrying my head off in this hotel room."

"Baby, you and I have already been over this. It's much safer there for you. Until we can make sense of this whole thing, I need you to stay there. If I have to worry about your well being, I won't be able to function right. I'll let you know the minute something turns up. In the meantime, you can say a prayer for all of us. Okay?"

"I'm already ahead of you on the prayer. I called to tell you that Lisa is out of the coma. Lisa's mother called me from the hospital."

"That's great baby. Thank God. Some good news for a change."

"Well it is for her, but bad for others."

"What do you mean?" asked Allen.

"She doesn't remember much, but she gave a statement to the police. Spook hit her. She doesn't remember the rape.

They're still waiting on the results from the rape kit. Her mother is happy that Lisa will be okay, but she's worried about Jason. He hasn't been the same. He's hanging out with young thugs and hardly goes to school anymore. He doesn't even know that his mother has come out of her coma."

"Yeah that's sad. When something like this happens, there's more than one victim. Loved ones are so deeply affected by the hurt and pain, mentally and physically. Prayerfully in time he'll bounce back."

"I wanted to give you a heads up. Spook is crazy, but he is your brother. I know you love him."

"Thanks Carol, I appreciate it. I'll call you soon so just stay put alright?"

Reluctantly she said, "Yes Allen."

"Promise me Carol."

"I promise."

"I love you."

"I love you too."

Allen put his phone in his coat pocket. He pulled into the hotel parking lot. How had things had gotten so out of hand? Everything was fine a week ago. He and Stone were making money and living a good life. They didn't hurt anyone or make any waves. They hadn't made so much as a ripple in the pond. Then along came a spider. Spook made tidal waves.

Spook had everyone stay one room while he talked to his brother in private. They cleaned up the hotel rooms. There were no drugs or paraphernalia in sight. Allen was aware that he got high, but to flaunt it before him was another thing. Besides, Spook never ever wanted to see his brother get involved in the dope game. He was proud of Allen for not getting mixed up in that vicious cycle. Keeping it out of his little brother's face was more out of respect than anything.

There was a knock at the door, Spook closed the adjoining door with Isis, Michelle, and Crack Pipe on the other side. Then he looked through the peep hole and saw Allen standing there. Spook opened the door and let him in. He quickly secured the door shut. They hugged and exchanged small pleasantries.

Both men sat down at the table. Allen looked directly in Spook's eyes. He said, "Lisa's awake. She identified you as the assailant. We both know how this works. They will be getting a warrant for you arrest. The rape kit results aren't back as of yet."

"Allen, just so you know, I punched her lights out. But on everything I love I didn't run up in her. No man should ever have to rape any woman for the pussy. It's too much out there being given away. You know that for yourself. I had hoe's on the stroll. Back in my day we had an unspoken rule among the real men of old school. Your game had to be strong by talking them out of their panties, not taking the pussy. You make love to the body and you rape their minds. Today they got the game all fucked up.

Believe me Allen, I'm not the one who raped her." said Spook. He looked in Allen's eyes.

Allen studied Spook for moment before saying, "I believe you."

Spook sighed, "I know that I've been on the rampage out here taking people's shit. I knew it would come to this. My plan is to get far from here anyway. Maybe I'll go to some island where they don't have extradition. Then I can lay back under a palm tree and sip umbrella drinks."

"Spook, I remember when I was younger and you went on the run. You told me it takes great deal of money. How do you plan on making it? I mean I'll give you the money that you need, but you didn't know that. What were your plans to getting the money?"

Spook went to the closet and brought out two big duffel bags. He sat them on the bed and unzipped them both. He motioned for Allen to come see. Allen walked over and looked down into the duffel bags. He saw money was stacked high in both bags.

Allen let a whistle escape his lips. "Damn Spook! You've been a very busy man."

"I have almost the same value of dope in the next room with my crew. Needless to say, I stepped on some toes getting it."

"I don't want to know. Just watch your back and be careful." Allen held up both hands as he went back to his seat.

216

Spook put away the bags and joined Allen at the table. He stated, "I will be leaving town tomorrow. I will contact you before I leave. You okay with that?"

"Yeah man. You better contact me before you leave."

"Listen Lil brother, I'm sorry for the way I acted and for what I said to you the last time you saw me. I'd never do anything to hurt you, but I would kill the man who tried."

"I believe you. It's behind us. Let's turn the page and shake on it," said Allen.

"Naw, fuck that! You better stand up and show me some brotherly love motha fucka."

The brothers hugged and patted each other on the back. An uneasy silence hung in the air for a moment. Spook broke the silence by saying, "I know I had you worried. You disagree with my methods, but I sense there's more. What's troubling you lil brother."

"Spook the other reason that I wanted to speak to you is to see if can help me out with something."

"Spill it."

"Do you know or have you heard of a guy out of Detroit named Herbert T?"

"I don't know him, but I know of him. He used to sell drugs and had his hand into whatever could make a buck. He was feared because of the rumors of the brutal ways he killed people. The cops never could pin anything on him."

"You should also know that Big Mama was Herbert T's sister."

Spook looked at him with surprise. "Ain't that a bitch?!? Dig that!"

Allen brought Spook up to speed on the confrontation with Herbert T. and No Neck Norman. He went on to tell him about Tomorrow, Stone, and Dwayne disappearing, the blood on the floor of the club, and him tucking Carol away for safety.

"Damn!" said Spook, "I guess that saying is true. Everything is connected. Here I was thinking I was the only one going through hell. You know I'm not crazy about your friends, especially that Stone, but I'll help you if I can. I'll fuck up this Herbert T. and his boys when it comes to you. So they're here in town, huh?"

Allen' phone rang just as he was about to answer Spook's question. Allen held up one finger to Spook, indicating for him to hold on a minute. It was one of his street contacts. He said, "Hello, tell me you have some good news."

Spook lit a cigarette and poured drinks for them. Allen seemed upset by the conversation.

"Alright. Thanks anyway. Let me know if something comes up. This is important," Allen said as he hung up. Allen placed his phone back in his pocket. Spook handed him a double shot of Cognac. Allen drank the smooth brown liquid.

"No one has seen Herbert T. or any of his crew. It's as if he's disappeared into thin air. You'd think someone would have seen or remembered seeing a powder blue Hummer."

Spook had just finished his drink. What Allen said about the Hummer hit him. "I saw a powder blue Hummer yesterday."

Allen's eyes lit up. He sat straight up in his chair. He couldn't ask the question fast enough. "Where?"

***

Stone's head felt like it was in a vise. He slowly opened his eyes. This had to be the monster of all headaches. He felt disoriented. Stone looked around and assessed his situation. He was on a concrete floor. A little bit of light filtered in under the crack of the door. The place was cold and smelled musky. He guessed he was in a small warehouse. He could see oil stains on certain parts of the floor where the light hit. He tried to stand only to find himself restrained by a greasy rope around his chest. He was tied to an iron pole. They had his hands and feet tied so tight he could hardly feel them. The ropes were cutting off his circulation.

No telling how long he would be alone, so he figured time would be best served trying to free himself. He tried working his hands and feet free. His attempts were in vain. The ropes wouldn't loosen one bit. Moving just made them bite into his flesh more.

He tried to think. The last thing he remembered was being struck in the back of the head by Dwayne, a man that he and Allen had come to respect and trust. Why didn't he see this coming? Dwayne had been acting different over the last several months.

All the while, he had been in league with the devil. Make that two devils, Dwayne and Herbert T. Stone's mind raced at the speed of light. Where was Tomorrow? Had Allen missed him yet? How long had he been out? Where was he? Where were his captors? How in the hell was he going to get out of this? The questions plagued him. Then he heard footsteps. A door opened. They were getting closer. Two male voices could be heard, but Stone couldn't make out what they said or who was talking. Suddenly, bright light flooded the room. It hurt his eyes. Stone could make out two forms as they stepped inside. Stone's eyes adjusted to the light. He could now see the two men. One wore braids while the other had a clean shaven head.

"Good, you're awake," said Bald head.

"Where am I?" asked Stone.

"You'll find out soon enough," said the man with the braids. He untied the rope around Stone's chest and helped him stand.

"Remove the rope from his feet. I ain't carrying him. Leave his hands tied," said Baldy.

"Don't try to run. We're miles from nowhere and no one can hear screams this far out. Do what you're told," demanded Braids.

Stone attempted to stand but it took a few minutes to adjust. Pin prick sensations went through his legs due to lack of blood circulation. Finally the feeling was coming back to his lower half. The two men walked Stone outside holding him by his arms. The sun was shining bright and it felt good on his face. The snow was all but gone.

It wasn't in a warehouse. He had been in a big pole barn that was away from the house that he was now being pushed and herded towards. He saw the powder blue Hummer in the driveway. He was taken through the back door and into the basement. The house was a nice size, really spacious. From what little Stone could see, it cost more than an average couple's income.

Stone was pushed roughly in a seat at the table while Braids and Bald head hovered directly behind him. Shortly afterwards, No Neck and Herbert T. came down the steps. They sat opposite Stone. Stone made a mental note that No Neck was wearing his twin .357 Mags. Herbert T. and No Neck poured themselves a drink. Herbert T. then lit a big cigar and chewed a bit on the end.

"Stoney boy, look at you now." said Herbert T trying to sound like Scarface from the movie. "Would you care for something to drink?"

"Where is Tomorrow?" asked Stone.

"She's been here for two days now. And very comfortable I must say. You should be more worried about yourself. I do, however, apologize for the crude accommodations. Never the less, I was hoping we could talk and still act like

221

sensible men. Of course, you'll remain in those restraints due to your violent tendencies. I wouldn't want my men to put a bullet in your brain before we had a chance to talk. Do you understand?" Herbert T. tried his best to sound sophisticated.

Stone took into account that Herbert T. was talking like this to taunt him.

"Where is Tomorrow? " Stone asked again.

"Okay, you want it like that. Fine, but hear me out Stoney boy. My new men wanted you dead. If it wasn't for me you'd be taking a dirt nap. I don't need you to find out that Allen's brother killed my sister. Trust me he's going to get his. The only reason you're still alive is because I want you to see your girl and I want her to see you. Before you die, I want to destroy you from the inside out. I want you to know what it feels like to have your heart torn out from your chest."

Stone tried to jump across the table at this idiot. He was forcefully pulled back into his seat by the two men behind him. No Neck was enjoying this. He lit a cigarette and threw the burnt out match at Stone.

Stone was enraged. "What have you done with her?"

Herbert T. started laughing loud and hard. When he stopped laughing, he downed the rest of his drink. Herbert T. studied Stone's face. "You think we raped her don't you?" He sat back in his chair, put his feet up on the table, and crossed one leg over the other. "Stoney boy, me and my boys may do some undesirable shit from time to time, but we are civilized men. We ain't no monsters. I assure you she was not defiled or deflowered, at least not while she's been with us. Now if she's got some dick elsewhere, that's for you to discuss. A fine ass woman like her, I wouldn't be surprised if it was another rooster in her hen house."

All of the men laughed at that. Stone felt a bit of relief, but then what did Herbert T. mean about destroying him from the inside out?

"I'm going to have them take you to where she is. I'll even give you two sometime together. Never let it be said that I don't have a heart. I'm going after your friend Allen and his brother. When I return, we all can have a talk. Now if you behave, I'll let you watch us torture Spook before I kill all of you. Dwayne told us you and Spook don't care for each other. All and all, it should be a nice get together."

"Where is that snake anyway?" asked Stone.

"Your Judas, is keeping an eye on Tomorrow. In fact, he's giving her some food. Come now, I know you've been dying to see her."

They led Stone through a long basement hallway. Herbert T. knocked on a steel door with a very small reinforced window. A metal cover was closed over the window. Dewayne opened the door. He stepped out, then closed the door. Stone wanted to bust his face up, but Braids and Bald Head held him back.

Dewayne said, "I had this special room built for people I wanted to have a long talk with. You'll find comfort in knowing it was your money that paid for this house and everything. I've been playing you and yo boy Allen like a deck of cards. Now it's time to play you both like Jeff, to the left. Thanks to both of you I have knowledge of your operations. I've always been smarter than you Stone, and I'll be a step ahead of you. Oh, by the way," He drew back and slapped Stone with the back of his hand reopening Stone's busted lip. "I always wanted to do that." Then he stepped away. Stone winced. Not because of the blow, more so because of Dwayne's foul breath.

"Now that Dwayne has got that off his chest, you should go to her. She's in there." said Herbert T. They opened the door and removed the rope from Stone's hands. They shoved him the room, slamming the door behind him. He was pushed so hard that he fell to the floor.

The room was dark and damp. Herbert T. and Dwayne watched through the window in the door. There was a cot in the corner of the room and a small table with candles burning on it. Stone saw movement on the cot. The person had their head bent down. Stone couldn't even make out the face in the candle light. Stone got to his feet and went to the little bed. This wasn't Tomorrow. Whoever this was, had scabs all over their head. More than likely due to someone rushing to shave the hair off. He saw track marks on both arms. The female slowly raised her head and looked up with empty dope fiend eyes. Slob was around her mouth.

Tomorrow spoke in a slurred voice. "Baby is ….
that…..you? I told them you….you'd …come for me."
She scratched at her neck.

Herbert T. and Dwayne laughed. Herbert T. managed to say, "I neglected to tell you that he has been feeding her dog food for days now." The two men continued laughing.

Dog food was the street name for Heroin. Stone covered his eyes with both hands trying to erase the harsh reality. He fell to his knees screaming, "NOOOOOOOOOOOO!"

CHAPTER 24

Spook brought Allen up to date on what happened to Herbert T's sister, the jack moves, the killings at the dope houses, and his dealings with Marty. Allen was amazed Spook made it through all of that alive. When they were coming up, Spook would get into some trouble but come out of it smelling like a rose. Allen didn't approve of what Spook and his new found friends did, but he was glad his brother hadn't been killed. Spook had his crew come into the room. He introduced Allen to Crack Pipe, Michelle, and Isis. To Allen's surprise, both women were stunningly beautiful. Both women were also naked. There was no shame in their game.

"Spook, you're so lucky. I bet you could piss in a swinging hot sauce bottle. Now get to the part about the Hummer please" Allen said.

Spook said, "I was getting to that part. Well anyway, after we left Marty's we headed back here. A few miles before we hit Battle Creek, I saw this nice house on a hill with a powder blue Hummer in a long driveway. It struck me as odd and out of place. It just didn't belong."

"Can you remember how to get back out there?"

"No, not really."

"Fuck!" Allen was frustrated.

"But I'm sure Michelle can get us there."

Allen felt some hope. His spirits lifted a bit. He gave thought to Spook's motley crew. They were dope fiends, women of the streets, thieves, and killers. If they did what Spook said they had done, it was a good guess that they all were psychopaths. Spook included. His brother had formed them to be his deadly tools. Maybe he could use their help after all. You had to be a little crazy to live in an insane world.

"Okay Spook. We need to get going; my mellow is out there probably hurt or dead. This whole thing is time sensitive. It's your show. How are we going to play it?"

"Look, you're my baby brother. I would die for you, but let's get something straight right now. I don't give a rat's ass about your mellow. They can butcher his pretty ass for all I care. I'm in this for you and only you Allen."

"All I need is for you to show me the spot. I can go in alone. I know how to handle myself. I have for all these years while you were in prison. Stone has really been there for me. He saved my ass more than once. I must be there for him."

"Fuck that! You're my lil brother. If a motha fucka fucks with you, he's fucking with me. Since Stone saved yo life, I figure I owe him since I wasn't there and he was. I'm going all the way with you on this one. Yo little peanut head ass ain't gonna stop me. Once we find yo boy, I'm gonna rob Herbert T's punk ass." Spook smiled. "I got two of the most gangster bitches this side of the Mexican border. Herbert T. gonna get his ass whipped, his money took, and his name put in the undertakers book."

"Okay, you finished? Can we go now?" asked Allen.

"Yes we can go, but before we do let me put you up on game. I know you're in a rush, but just hear me out. I've been doing this shit way longer than you. I was doing this shit when our parents were hustling up money for diapers for yo ass. To come out of this on top, you've got to come out of your way of thinking. You and Stone have money and are real soft and comfortable with good living. There's nothing wrong with that as long as you are out of the game. You ain't hungry no more. Now the buzzards are circling, waiting for yo asses to drop so they can pick bones clean. Let me show you something."

Spook brought out the plastic explosives with the timer still attached. Allen's eyes got big. He stepped away from Spook.

"Oh hell naw! I know that ain't what I think it is." said Allen.

"You dam right it is. It's C4, compliments of Marty. I'm gone do them motha fucka's before they do me."

"Man is that shit safe?"

"It won't detonate unless I push this button or set the timer. Relax and stay focused."

"I just hope you know what the fuck you're doing with that shit. Another thing, Spook, we must still be careful of 5-0. I'm sure they have a warrant out for you by now. " said Allen with concern.

"One problem at a time lil brother," replied Spook.

Spook turned his attention to Isis, Michelle and Crack Pipe.

"Get some clothes on. We're still going to Detroit, but we got to take care of some business with my brother first. Crack Pipe, pack up your hardware. You bitches get both of these rooms in order. Don't leave anything."

They all moved with purpose. Allen liked how they followed Spook's orders. It was plain to see that Spook disciplined his crew. The naked women were on the bed and the one called Crack Pipe was on the floor. If the situation wasn't so serious, Allen would have allowed himself to be distracted by watching the women play with each other's pussies. They stopped what they were doing when Spook issued orders. Most dopers would have kept on getting high. Allen noticed Spook eyeing him.

"The guys you're going up against are deadly serious about taking you and you boy down. Let me school you before they fool you. You must get in the mind frame of your enemies. Know that you can't be as good as they are. You must be better than them. Lives depend on it. Now let's do some simple math. You have to ask yourself, what is the common denominator of this equation?"

Spook continued, "From what you've told me, Herbert T. has been some steps ahead of you the whole time. Think about that for a minute. That nigga ain't from this way, which leads me to believe he's getting some help from someone. Whoever it is has been hemorrhaging information for some time. It's someone who knows you

229

and Stone dealings. Be it a man or a woman, it's someone who you both trust."

"That sounds kind of thin Spook. I doubt that anyone in this town has an axe to grind with me or Stone. We treat people well and we pay people well," said Allen.

"Who said they were from Battle Creek? The most obvious question is who has the most to gain with you and yo boy Stone out of the picture, other than Herbert T.?"

Allen took a long moment to think about what Spook said. He couldn't think of anyone.

Spook yelled, "Come on Allen! Start thinking like a predator instead of the prey motha fucka!"

Allen stiffened his back as though he had been stabbed in it. "Wait a damn minute!" Allen was excited. He jumped from his chair. "Naw, it can't be. No way!"

Spook interrupted him. "Who? It could be."

"Dwayne. He knows our operations in and out. I find it hard to believe that he…"

Spook stood, walked over to Allen and put of his hands on his brother's shoulders. He looked him square in the eyes. "Wake up to the real world Allen. Just because you've put Dwayne in a good position and looked out for him don't mean shit. At least not to him. Maybe it's him, maybe it's not. Don't be blind to human nature. Greed! If you give a snake a mouse, he'll still ask you for a beer to wash it down. Just call him to check and see if he's heard anything on Stone. See if you detect anything. Remember, you are the predator and he is your prey."

Everything Spook said made good sense. Why hadn't Allen called Dwayne when he found out Stone was missing? If Dwayne was a traitor, maybe it was a good thing he didn't. Now he wanted to call and confirm Spook's theory. Allen pulled out his cell phone and called Dwayne.

***

Dwayne and Herbert were in the Hummer on their way to Allen's house. They hoped he would lead them to Spook. Bald Head, Braids, and No Neck stayed at the house with Stone and Tomorrow. The powder blue Hummer made its way down the road. Dwayne barley heard his phone ring over the loud music. Dwayne turned the music down. He told Herbert T. not to say anything because it was Allen calling. He answered, "Hey Allen. Where you at?"

"I'm in the car with my baby. Where are you?" Allen replied.

"I'm heading back to the club. Have you guys heard anything on Tomorrow?"

"No not yet. Is Stone with you? He's not answering his phone."

"Naw, I left him at the club. We met up with Herbert T. Everything went fine. Stone convinced Herbert T. to back off and he assured Stone that it must have been someone else who took Tomorrow. Maybe he's out looking for Tomorrow."

"Okay I was just checking with you. I'll call you later," said Allen.

"Hey Allen, I have something that you need to know. I need to see you face to face. What I have to say shouldn't be said over the phone. Can you meet me at the club?"

Allen was burning mad, but tried not to let Dwayne know it. He had found the mole. "Yeah, no problem. Let's say about ninety minutes. Does that work for you?"

"I was hoping it could be sooner. It's real important."

"Let me drop Carol off. I'll try to make it soon. If I'm a little behind on time, wait for me."

"I'll be there. I guess I can catch up on some paper work while I wait."

"Cool. Call me back if I haven't made it there in an hour, alright?"

"That'll work."

The line disconnected and Allen put his phone away. Spook knew that look on his brother's face. He'd seen it many times. When Allen was mad like this, he could be dangerously unpredictable.

"That motha fucka!" said Allen. "He wants to get me to the club."

"Let's go fuck up their plans," said Spook. He was ready to run out the door.

"No. Let them wait there. Let's go to the house where you saw the Hummer.   Every minute may count."

Spook agreed with Allen. They all got in Spook's van. Spook drove with Allen in the passenger seat. Michelle,Isis, and Crack Pipe sat in the back. Michelle gave directions. As they made their way down the back roads, Allen lookied out the window. He got madder by the minute.

"That motha fucka!" was all that Allen could bring himself to say.

CHAPTER 25

Stone sat on the cot with Tomorrow. He held her head to his chest. His emotions bubbled up inside him to see her like this. There wasn't a damn thing he could do about it. The wounds they inflicted upon him paled in comparison to the mental anguish he was experiencing.

Tomorrow would wake up for a minute from her drug induced stupor and then go back into her nod. The heroin was still in her system. Stone cried as he rocked her back and forth. Whoever shaved her hair off wasn't careful with the razor. Deep gouges of her skin had been shaved away with her hair. How could someone have been so cruel? She curled up in the fetal position.

Although he had been stripped of his phone and weapons, they had left him with his long winter coat. Tomorrow on the other hand, wore only a shirt and pants. It was damp and cold down here. Stone removed his coat and covered her with it. He tried to think of a way to get the two of them out of this mess. Bald Head and Braids would come to the small window in the door from time to time to check on them.

No Neck, Bald head, and Braids were upstairs playing poker for the moment. Tomorrow was awake. She watched Stone pace back and forth through the flickering candle light.

She cried, "Stone ..... Baby!"

Stone hurried to her side. "I'm here baby," he said. Stone sat on the bed next to her. Then he put her hand into his.

"I'm so sorry baby. I should have kept right on packing. We wouldn't be here now."

"Honey, this isn't your fault. Don't blame yourself. Herbert T. is from my past. If it wasn't for me, you wouldn't be in this mess."

"Stone you didn't make anyone do this to me. Those evil men are bound to get what's coming to them."

Just then a face appeared at the little window. It was No Neck. "Hey Tomorrow, you want some dog food?" He snickered.

She looked to Stone as if to ask permission to have it. Stone knew that puppy dog look and intervened. "Naw, she's okay."

Tomorrow said, "No I'm not. Soon I'll begin to hurt without it. They made me beg for it before you got here."

"Tomorrow, look at me. You can beat this."

She sniffled and put her arms around Stone's neck. "Okay. Stone please forgive me."

"I love you Tomorrow."

"I love you too."

"Oh ain't that touching? I'll leave you two work it out. I'll back in a few minutes," said No Neck.

Stone took Tomorrow's face into hands and kissed her. He looked into her eyes. "Baby you must not give in to that poison."

She said, "Stone let's not disillusion ourselves. I am now a dope fiend. Without it, I hurt. I love you so much. This is not what I wanted for us and this isn't how it was suppose to be. I could never be your wife now. Look at me. I'm a disgrace. I'm a sea hag with a habit."

Stone looked at this woman he loved and admired. This is what Herbert T. meant by destroying him from the inside out. Stone felt as though his heart was being ripped from his chest.

"Tomorrow we can get though this together. Baby, we can beat this. I've been there and done that. They forced those drugs on you. You didn't have a choice. Please baby, I'll help you get through this. Nothing has changed. When we get out of here, we'll get you detoxed and move on with her our lives. I still want you as my wife and mother of my children." He pressed his lips to hers.

She kissed him back, cherishing his touch. She looked into his eyes with tears running down her face. "Oh Stone, I'm so in love with you. Yes baby, I'll try. I'll do anything for you. I'll always love you."

Suddenly the door flew open. Stone's back was to it. The bald headed man and the man with the braids grabbed Stone by the arms and pulled him away from Tomorrow. No Neck entered with a small canvas bag. He pushed

Tomorrow flat on the bed, unzipped the bag, and brought out a syringe with brown liquid in it.

Tomorrow started to cry. "Please no more. Please don't. No more."

Stone knew it was more heroin. He quickly pulled his right arm free from the man with braids and tried to lunge at No Neck. The bald headed man tackled Stone. Braids helped him wrestle Stone to the floor. Their fist and feet rained down on Stone's head, side, back, and stomach.

Bald Head said, "Herbert T. only gave us two rules. One, we couldn't rape your girl and two, we're not suppose to kill you. He didn't say that we couldn't kick yo ass and beat the shit out of you. If you try something like that again, I'll start cutting on her. I cut this bitch in Detroit. I cut that bitch up like a Thanksgiving turkey, right there on the streets. Anyway, I'm suppose to make you watch. Don't close your eyes. If you do, I'll cut your eyelids off so you'll have to watch. Now behave yourself or I'll start slicing."

No Neck held the syringe up to the candle light, making sure the dosage of heroin was right and there was no air bubbles in the syringe.

"Wait, don't do this to her," said Stone. He was in pain from the beating and the knee that was pressed hard to his back.

"Orders are Orders," said No Neck. He grabbed Tomorrow's arm and held the needle close to her skin.

Stone never felt so helpless. "Please, don't do it to her. Give it to me. I'll do whatever you ask. Please, I'm begging you man. Don't put any more of that junk into her," pleaded Stone. Sweat ran down his forehead and the veins could be seen swelling in his neck.

"Oh, I'm sorry Stone. You've mistaken me for someone who gives a fuck," said No Neck. He rammed the needle in Tomorrow's arm. Tomorrow slowly relaxed. No Neck removed the needle. They all watched the drug take effect. Her eyes glazed over. She felt no pain as she went into her nod. Bald Head pulled his gun. Herbert T's men backed out the door. They slammed it shut and locked it loudly.

Stone winced from the pain in his side and back. It felt like a couple of his ribs were broken. He managed to get up from the floor. He limped over to the cot. Damn them. He wanted to kill them for what they did to her. He knew how it felt to be strung out and dependent on drugs. He didn't wish that on anyone. His was major concern was getting her out alive.

Tomorrow was aware of Stone's presence. She opened her arms to him and they hugged. She did her best to talk coherently. "Tell Carol... thanks for being a .... And thank...You for being so wonderful to....me."

"Baby, don't talk like that, we are going to make it out of this and you can tell Carol yourself," replied Stone.

She had nodded out again. Stone wasn't sure if she even heard him.

CHAPTER 26

No Neck Norman, Bald Head, and Braids were playing poker and smoking weed when they heard a vehicle in the driveway. No Neck looked out the window. He saw was a white woman approaching the door. She was a cute blond and carried a small brief case. Her hair was in a pony tail and she was dressed in business attire. She knocked on the door. No Neck ordered the men to put their guns and weed away. He figured the incense they burned would mask the smell of the weed.

Braids opened the door. He used his polite voice, but was ready to draw his gun just in case. "Hello. How may I help you Miss?"

"Hi, I'm Mrs. Applebee, and I'm with the neighborhood watch council. We're holding a meeting tomorrow at our local church. We are going door to door inviting new people in this area to come. Bring the whole family," she said.

Braids couldn't keep his eyes off her cleavage. Her top was very low cut. It allowed him to see portion of her nice ripe melons. Braids was mesmerized with her. He just stood there with the door wide open. She saw the two men at the table with the cards, liquor bottles, and cigarette filled ashtrays.

"Hey man," Braids said over his shoulder, "She's with some neighborhood watch group."

"We can hear. Do you think we are deaf?" asked No Neck.

No Neck figured he better handle this. They must appear to be normal men doing normal things. The last thing they needed was the police out here. Black folks this far out would surely raise some eyebrows. Having two people kidnapped in the basement would be pretty hard to explain. He'd better play it cool.

"Miss, the owner of the home is away on business. Me and my friends are house sitting." No Neck gave her his best smile.

If my timing is bad, I should come back another day," said Mrs. Applebee. "You gentlemen have a good day." She walked away with a sexy walk.

Braids eyes were glued to her ass. The motion of her ass was hypnotic. He watched as she took each step. She stopped, turned around, and walked back to the door.

"Silly me. Forgive my manners. Will you please give the owner my card?" she asked.

"Sure," said Braids. He held out his hand to receive the card.

She balanced her brief case on her bent knee and opened it. Braids had a full bird's eye view of her cleavage. He watched her breasts as she shuffled papers. When her hand came out, he was staring down the barrel of her gun. The surprise made him take a lung full of air and his eyes went buck wide.

Michelle's gun exploded. The bullet drilled a hole right through Braids left eye. Braids was dead before he hit the floor. No Neck and Bald Head moved quickly in different directions. Bald Head dived behind the couch while No Neck tipped the table over for cover and crawled towards one of the back rooms.

That was the signal they were waiting for. Spook and Allen ran to the door with their guns out. Michelle continued to fire at Bald head and No Neck. Her shots went wild as they escaped out of her line of fire.

Spook and Allen came through the door, low and fast. They bumped her out of the way. "One is hiding behind the couch and the other ran to the back," Michelle said.

"Okay. Good job. Now go to the van with the rest. Watch our backs and be sure to let us know if anyone comes. Go!" demanded Spook.

Wood chips flew as a bullet went past Allen and hit the door frame. Allen took cover behind a Lazy Boy chair. Spook saw the muzzle flash from the gun.

"You okay little brother?" asked Spook.

"Yeah. How about you?" answered Allen.

"So far so good. Watch your back. I 'm going to flush out a roach."

Spook made his way silently along the hallway. Spook knew which room the shot came from. If he went in there now, he would surely catch some hot lead. Spook grabbed a picture from the wall and hurled it into the room. Gun shots exploded. Spook imagined the look on the man's face once he realized that he just killed a picture. Spook rushed into the room. He fired from his hip at the movement to his left. Two bullets came from the .357 twin Pythons that No Neck had taken from Stone. The first shot went wild, but the second went through the sleeve of Spook's coat barley missing Spook's arm.

No Neck wasn't as fortunate. The .45 slug from Spook's Desert Eagle caught him in the shoulder. He spun around and dropped his guns. He held his wound and slid down the wall into a sitting position. No Neck's face was contorted with pain. Spook placed the barrel of his gun to the man's forehead.

Allen heard five shots from the back room. His heart was racing and his hands were sweaty. "You, behind the couch. I just want my friend and his girl. You don't matter to me. Just tell me where they are and you can leave here alive," said Allen.

"Motha fucka, you ain't running shit but yo mouth. You don't know who you fucking with," said the man.

Then he held the gun over the couch, aimed it in Allen's directions and fired 3 quick shots hoping to hit Allen. The Shots went nowhere near Allen.

"Fuck this shit!" Allen yelled. He stood up from behind the chair and fired his .44 Mag into the couch.

Bullet after bullet tore through the couch like a hot knife through butter. Bald Head took off. He shot behind him as he ran. He wasn't really aiming to hit anything. It was just to distract Allen long enough so he could get to a better shooting position. His back was to Allen. Allen took careful aim and didn't give him the time to get off another shot. The first. 44 hollow point hit Bald Head in his neck, crushing and tearing apart his spine. The second tore through his back and punched a hole through his lung. He fell in front of No Neck and Spook.

The sudden movement at Spook's feet startled him. He didn't know what was happening. Survival mode kicked in and he shot the already dead man twice in the head.

The head exploded into a bloody pulp. No Neck was horrified. He held his bleeding shoulder. He trembled. Not just from seeing what happened to Bald Head, but more so because Spook now had his deadly weapon pointed at his face.

Spook asked, "Allen, You good out there?"

"Yeah. Spook are you hurt?" Allen answered.

"Right as rain. Don't shoot. I'm bringing one out with me."

No Neck stopped and looked down at what once was a whole man at his feet. It wasn't long ago that he was playing cards and smoking weed with his old friend. Spook slapped No Neck across the back of his head with his gun. Wham!

"Keep your gun on him Allen. I like the guns he dropped in that room," said Spook. He went to retrieve the guns.

Allen took a good look at No Neck. "Where is Stone, Bitch ass motha fucka?"

"Man I'm bleeding to death. Get me to the hospital and I'll tell you everything you want to know," pleaded No Neck.

Allen cocked his gun. He gave a deadly look and said, "Motha Fucka, tell me now or die!"

"Okay, Okay!" cried No Neck.

"Those are Stone's," Allen said with excitement when he saw Spook holding the Pythons. He directed his attention back to No Neck and pointed his gun at his manhood. "Where is he?"

"Downstairs in the basement," No Neck said breathing hard.

"Who else is in the house?" Spook interjected.

"Y'all killed everyone else but me. Herbert T. left us here to watch Stone and that bitch. Man, I told you he's downstairs. Now get me some medical help man."

Spook shouted, "Shut the fuck up! You think we trust yo short ass? You're leading the way down them steps and if there are any surprises, I'm gonna put two to the back of yo head. Now lead the way Motha fucka. Look at you bleeding all over the place."

"Spook, let me get those guns. I'm going to shut that front door before we go downstairs," said Allen.

Spook gave him the guns. Allen went to the door and saw Isis, Michelle, and Crack Pipe looking through the van's window. Allen gave them the thumbs up and shut the door. They went down the steps with their guns out and No Neck in the lead.

CHAPTER 27

Stone was doing his best to comfort Tomorrow when he heard the first gun shots. What the hell was going on up there? Tomorrow jumped when she heard the gun fire. Stone didn't know what to make of it. Maybe it was the police coming to their rescue or maybe it was some of Herbert T's enemies. The Machiavellian saying came to mind. The enemy of my enemy is my friend.

Stone knew that he couldn't just sit there. He quickly made up his mind. When they opened the door, he would charge whoever came in and try to overpower them. "Who I am kidding?" he thought to himself. His ribs were either cracked or broken. He wasn't fit for battle.

Sure enough the door opened. There stood No Neck holding his shoulder. Stone was getting ready to spring for him when Spook and Allen came into view. Stone exhaled in relief. He never guessed it could be them. Spook and Allen looked at Stone and Tomorrow. Allen ran pushed No Neck to the floor when he ran to Stone. No Neck cried out in pain. Stone and Allen hugged each other.

"Are y'all alright?" asked Allen.

"I'm a bit beat up, but I can make it. I'm more concerned about her," replied Stone.

"Hello Allen. I'm not so hot," said Tomorrow.

Allen couldn't believe his eyes. This didn't even look like Tomorrow. This woman looked like a frog peeping through ice.

"Hi Tomorrow. Sorry we couldn't get here any sooner," said Allen.

Before Allen could ask, Stone said, "They cut her hair off and been pumping her up with that dog for days now. Her body has become dependent on it." Stone looked at Spook with gratitude. "I owe you big for this. Thanks."

Spook said, "Don't thank me. Thank Allen. If it weren't for him, you'd still be locked up down here."

"How did you know where we were Allen?" Stone asked.

"Come on upstairs. We'll fill each other in on what we do and don't know. Hopefully we can put a solution together. Spook, take No Neck upstairs and tie his ass to a chair. We need some info on Herbert T," said Allen. "Here Stone, I've got a gift for you."

Allen handed Stone his two .357 Pythons. Stone grabbed them and looked at them. He felt more comfortable with them in his hands. He tucked them in the waistband of his pants near the small of his back. They helped Tomorrow to her feet. They all started for the door when Tomorrow stopped in her tracks.

"Stone honey, I'm no good for you anymore. I love you enough to let you go on with your life," said Tomorrow with dismay in her voice. "baby don't talk like that, we're going to get you fixed up. Those are the drugs talking, hang in there you're going home with me." Replied Stone. "Carol is waiting to see you." Added Allen. The stairs was too narrow for them all to go up at once. Allen went up first, while Stone was ushering Tomorrow, she spun around Stone grabbing one of his guns. Tomorrow placed the device of death under her left breast and cocked the hammer back. "TOMORROW NO!" Yelled Stone. Allen turned heading back down the stairs, Tomorrow was backing down the steps as Stone walked slowly towards her. "Stone thank you for being a part of my life. I'll always love you. God please forgive me!" "Tomorrow please listen to..." She pulled the trigger that ended her life as her limp body fell to the floor. Stone felt so numb he couldn't cry. Apart of him felt like he had died with her. He bent down and held her in his arms saying a silent prayer, then stood and turned around standing straight not holding his ribs any more.

Spook yelled down the steps, "Is everything alright?"

Allen said, "No, but we're coming up."

Stone checked the clip on both guns. Stone stomped up the steps with the guns in both hands. Allen decided that it was best not to say anything to him now.

Spook had tied No Neck to a chair in the kitchen and had gagged him. Stone walked up to No Neck and knocked him and the chair to the floor. He pistol whipped No Neck without mercy. All No Neck could do was moan and grunt from the blows. Stone finally stopped hitting him. He cocked both hammers on both guns as he stood over the beaten man. Spook and Allen both knew that Stone would shoot him but they said nothing.

Suddenly a change came over Stone. "Naw motha fucka, I'm not done with you yet." He sat No Neck and his chair back in the sitting position and removed the gag. "Where the hell is Herbert T.?" asked Stone. No Neck said nothing.

Allen motioned for Stone to follow him in the other room. Spook kept an eye on No Neck. Allen explained how he thought Dwayne had been acting odd lately and brought Stone up to date on what he knew. Stone also told Allen about Dwayne and what he knew.

"Let's go meet Dwayne at the club. This guy will talk but we don't have time," said Stone.

They went back into the kitchen. Allen said, "We should be leaving Spook."

"So what y'all gone with this sorry motha fucka?" asked Spook.

"Listen, I can help y'all. I know everything about Herbert T. I'll give you all the information that you need. Please don't kill me," pleaded No Neck.

Stone looked him square in the eyes. "I begged you not to shoot that shit in Tomorrow's arm. You laughed and did it anyway. She was out of her head on that shit you gave her. She took her own life."

"I'm sorry man. I was 1 under orders. Herbert T. wanted you to see her suffer. It wasn't personal man."

"That's where you're wrong. It is personal to me. She was the purest thing in my life. You helped take her away from me."

Allen and Spook could see the hurt in Stone's eyes and heard it in his voice. Allen hoped he wouldn't be mentally scarred for the rest of his life. Either way he'd be there for him.

"Come on man. You sucker stroking over a dope fiend bitch. Man I'll hook you up with some hoes and help you bring Herbert T's ass down. All I ask is that you please don't kill me. Do we have a deal Stone?"

"I'm sorry. You've mistaken me for someone who gives a fuck," said Stone with a twisted smirk on his face.

Stone fired both guns twice. All four of the projectiles found their marks. No Neck was hit in his chest and stomach. Droplets of No Neck's blood peppered Stone's face.

"Stone, we should be going. What do we do with Tomorrow?" asked Allen.

"She's dead. Her spirit is gone. Her body is just an empty shell now. Leave it here," said Stone. He hung his head.

"I'll do clean up," Spook stated. He hugged Stone. Allen liked what he was seeing.

Then Spook went over to stove and disconnected the gas line. It made a hissing sound. The odor of the gas was strong. Spook set the bed on fire in the back bedroom. He walked out quickly closing the door. All three men wasted no time running to the van. Allen drove, Stone took the passenger seat, and Spook went in the back with his crew.

Spook looked out the window at the house to make sure they made a clean getaway. He saw the house burst into flames. Then he saw something that he didn't like. "Oh hell naw!" Spooked yelled.

Crack Pipe was picking at the floor. Spook looked at Isis and Michelle. They wouldn't meet his eyes. They were guilty of something. "I know you bitches ain't getting high while on a mission," said Spook. He was pissed.

"Baby, we only did a little. We kept a watch like you told us," said Isis in her little girl voice.

"Bitch, I don't give a fuck. All of y'all gone be dealt with when we get to ourselves. Right now we have business to take care of. Crack Pipe get yo tweaking ass off the floor and sit down somewhere," demanded Spook.

Crack Pipe looked like a child who got caught with his hand in the cookie jar. He did as he was told. Stone knew the vicious cycle of addiction. He felt no sorrow for them, but he did however feel empathy. He had been there.

Stone turned around to face the addicts who had saved his life. He said, "I extend my thanks to all of you for saving my life. I want all of you to know that if there is anything I can do for you, please feel free to call on me."

"Thanks, but no thanks. Me and my crew are set. Once we do Herbert T., we're out of this one horse town and on our way to "The D". I'm sorry for the loss of your girl," said Spook.

"Spook, I'm aware that Herbert T. is looking to put some lead into your ass for doing his sister. I got a beef with his ass too. So if I see him first, don't get in the way," Stone said.

"My baby didn't have anything to do with her death. I cut that fat bitch's throat with my glass pipe. Fuck that ho," said Isis.

"Yeah, and I shot that bitch afterwards. Damn that dick wearing bitch," added Michelle.

"Both of y'all shut the fuck up. Us men were talking. Who the fuck asked y'all? I can speak for myself. Anyway, I'm still pissed, so just shut the fuck up. I'm just two seconds from beating y'all asses," barked Spook.

"Spook, lighten up man," added Allen.

"Don't tell me to lighten up. When these motha fuckas get to slippin I don't lighten up. I tighten up."

Allen decided to leave it alone. In Spook 's line of work, a slip could cost him his life. He knew what he was doing.

"Yeah, my baby loves us. That's why he gets on us like that. He cares so ..." Isis didn't get to finish her sentence.

Without warning, Spook backhanded Isis across her face. The blow caused her head to spin in the opposite direction. "Didn't I tell you to shut the fuck up? Don't let me have to say it again."

Isis forced a half hearted smile and nodded her head yes. Stone had seen it too many times. They truly loved Spook. Not just because of the dope, but there was a deeper love as well. It was based on the attention. Many children were the same way. The need for attention caused them to get into trouble at home, the streets, school, or with the law. It was negative, but never the less, it was attention.

"I find it hard to believe Dwayne has been going behind our backs all this time. What he did to you and Tomorrow is unbelievable." Allen changed the subject.

"Do you think he's still waiting at the club?" asked Stone.

"I'm not sure. I told him it may take a while. That was more than an hour ago," replied Allen.

They went over what should be done as they neared the club. Stone, Spook and Michelle waited with anticipation as Allen, Isis, and Crack Pipe entered the club. Allen was directing this show.

Stone was impatient. He was glad they had stopped and replenished everyone's ammo. He checked both of his guns and nodded his head to Spook. Spook nodded back. They exited the van with Michelle on their heels. Allen, Isis, and Crack Pipe came back out the club. Stone wondered what the hell was going on.

"No one's in there. It's went from bad to worse," said Allen. He went in his pocket and handed a folded piece of paper to Stone.

Stone read it with Spook over his shoulder reading it with him. Stone heart skipped a beat.

Spook shouted, "What the fuck?"

***

The slap to her jaw stung something awful, sending her over the desk, taking papers, an ash tray, and lamp to the floor with her. Strong hands pulled her to her feet. She lashed out with her long nails, taking pieces of the man's skin as she dug deep into Herbert T's face. He winced at the stinging pain and slapped her again. She dropped like a sack of potatoes, Herbert t lifted his foot to stomp her. She screamed. Dwayne quickly stopped him."That's enough man, we need the bitch alive!" Dwayne shouted in the face of Herbert T. Herbert T gave her a mean look then went to fix himself up. Dwayne helped the female up and sat her down. They were at a warehouse not far from the club in the upstairs office. Dwayne had secretly bought this place on the side. "What the hell did you and that man take me from my house for? I would have never let you guys in if you hadn't said Stone was hurt and wanted to see me. I opened my door, and before I knew it the both of you were pushing me into some S.U.V. I know you work for Stone, could you tell me what this is all about? Am I being held for ransom?" Asked Delsena. "It's true, Stone does want to see you. No he's not hurt yet, yes we may hold you for ransom. Honestly right now you're bait." Replied Dwayne. "I see, your using me to get to Stone. You two brought me here and when I try to leave that man starts slapping me. Can i see Stone now?" "No you may not, as I said your bait." "Bait huh? We all know what happens to bait. I insist you take me to see Stone now." Demanded Delsena. "You will just be a good girl and you won't encounter no more pain." Said Herbert T butting into the conversation as he stood in the doorway of the office, patting his newly scratched face with a towel. Herbert t and Dwayne called Allen, and also called to the house where Stone and Tomorrow were being held and no one answered their phones, that couldn't have been a coincidence. They had to assume Allen was up on their game so they did the next best thing, they went after Allen's girl, Carol.

When they couldn't find Carol, they desperately looked through the phone numbers from the cell phone taken from Stone. Even his mother was fair game but couldn't be found by Herbert T's boys. Delsena's number was found, Dwayne called telling her that Stone was hurt and needed to see her. Dwayne took a seat behind the desk, across from Delsena, who was rubbing her face where she was slapped. Herbert T. was pacing the floor. "What did you ever see in Stone? A fine piece like you could have any man you want, plus you connected to big bucks."Questioned Dwayne. "So I guess I could have done better with you." replied Delsena, looking at Dwayne with distaste. "I like a woman with fire in her. I've seen you two love birds together and I would undress you with my eyes many times."Said Dwayne as he lit a cigarette. "Dwayne, you're fully aware that I'm in love with Stone, so why are we having this conversation?" "In love huh, although you know he's got a hard on for that dope fiend Tomorrow." "Yes, I will always love Stone, no matter what. As for Tomorrow she don't use drugs you must be mistaken." Delsena reasoned. Dwayne gave her the short version of what had taken place with Stone and Tomorrow.

255

Delsena listened with shock and disbelief. She found it hard to accept , saying " That poor girl, with her hands to her face. Tears began to come down her face when he got to the part about Stone. "And when Stone and Allen fall, their demise will bring about my rise to power. We will be in charge, I'll be rich with you as my queen, there will be nothing to stop us."Dwayne said with pride. "Dwayne, the thing with you and me it's just not going to happen. Your treachery with Stone and Allen is appalling, to violate their allegiance after all that they've done for you I find that sicking." Spat Delsena. Dwayne slammed his fist down on the desk in front of Delsena hard, causing her to jump. "Bitch I'm tired being nice and cordial, like it or not when all of this is over said and done, you and me will stain my bed. We will use you as leverage to ensure that Stone will bite the bait." She felt like scratching his eyes out, but knew that could prove to be futile. Herbert T. stopped pacing and looked at Dwayne. "We haven't heard from Allen, and Spook is still walking around alive. I want that son of a bitch dead for what he did to my sister."Said Herbert T. with much anger in his voice. "Relax motha fucka. Your hatred of Spook has blinded you and will be your down fall, if you don't put it in check. Everything happens in good time. I'm trying to show yo ass how we can take their money, their business, and their lives. Calm yo blood thirsty ass down and let me run the show here. I know what I'm doing," said Dwayne.

Herbert T. asked, "So what's our next move, man with the plan?"

"We try calling again. We pretty much know what happened, but let's go through the motions to be sure."

"You don't think we should at least drive past the house and see what's up for ourselves?" asked Herbert T.

Dwayne said, "Hell naw! You must be out of yo rabbit ass mind. For all we know the place is crawling with the cops. That damn pimped out powder blue Hummer of yours sticks out like a hard dick."

"Well how the fuck you plan on us making moves? You're out yo rabbit ass mind if you think I'm gonna walk."

"We won't have to. You think because I have been playing the sucker part that I didn't have no boys of my own? My boys are bringing my Lexus as we speak. They both are street conditioned and will do what I say. I'll have them both ride out and see what's going on out at the house after I get my car. Now, let's try to get a bead on Allen and Stone.

"This is insane. Listen to you. You're actually plotting to hurt people. Don't you know that violence begets violence? Why not just quit while you're ahead and abandon this foolishness before more people get hurt. Turn yourselves in. I'm sure they will go light on you. "said Delsena

Herbert T. and Dwayne looked at each other, Dwayne was thinking it, but Herbert T. said it. "Is this bitch serious?"

Herbert T. pulled out his switch blade, flicked it open, and walked towards Delsena with a wicked look on his face. Delsena cringed at the sight of the blade.

CHAPTER 29

All of them returned to the van. Stone found himself reading the note over again. YO GIRL DELSENA LOOKS AND SMELLS GOOD!

"Who the fuck is Delsena?" asked Spook.

"She's Stone's woman," said Allen.

"I thought Tomorrow was... Never mind."

"It's a long story Spook, but it's one I'm sure that you can relate to," said Stone. He looked at Isis and Michelle.

Spook understood.

"You think Herbert T. knows that you're onto him?" Spook asked Allen.

"I'd have to say yes to that question. I've missed several calls. Most likely Dwayne is one of them."

"What I'd like to know is how in the hell is Herbert T. always a step ahead of us. Now he has Del and no telling what she's being put through. I've got find her." said Stone.

***

"Yeah hello. Allen I see you've been a busy." "Yeah I'm a busy man, I have businesses' to run plenty for me to do. I went by the club and you weren't there. Said Allen trying to keep his composure." "Let's cut the bull Allen, I know Stone is with you. And I know you guys found my note, you should know that I'm a very serious individual, and I'm

not to be taken lightly. Put Stone on the phone."
"Demanded Herbert T. Allen handed Stone the phone."
"Stone speaking." "So you weaseled your way out of that
one Stoney boy huh?" "Let me speak to Delsena," Stone
demanded through the phone.

Herbert T. replied, "Whoa, slow down there Stoney Boy. I
want Spook. Then you can have Delsena."

"Let me speak to her first."

"As you wish." Herbert T. placed the phone to Del's ear.

She said, "Stone is that you?"

"Yeah baby, I'm coming to get you, stay calm," said Stone.

"Stone I…"

Herbert T. snatched the phone from her ear. "I want you to
bring me Spook," demanded Herbert T.

"Listen, nothing, and I do mean nothing better be wrong
with her. I promise you will die a slow death with much
agony," warned Stone.

"You are not in any position to make any threats. I'll call
you back shortly to tell you where you can bring that black
ass nigga that killed my sister. Someone would like to say
hello." He handed the phone to Dwayne.

"Hey Stone no hard feelings, right?" said Dwayne.

"Dwayne, what made you cross me likes this? I mean I
treated you with the utmost respect and gave you things

like you were a brother of mine. Now you do this to me? If Del gets hurt, take my word, I will kill you dead. Do you hear me?"

"Yeah I hear you Stone. She's okay, I stopped Herbert T from going at her with his knife. As long as you do what I say she will live. It's simple. Herbert T wants Spook and I want the businesses you and Allen have. You can have her back and there will be no more bloodshed.

"Tomorrow's dead. Three of our boy are dead. We'll call it even. You're really not in any position to make any demands or to tell me anything. I've worked for you guys for years, I know the operation and I know how you two think. Don't even try none of that monkey ass shit. I have the upper hand now. Do you hear me?"

"Yeah," answered Stone.

"Good." Dwayne ended the call.

Stone wanted to break something or someone. He was heated. "To make a long story short, he'll call us back and tell us where he wants to meet," said Stone. He looked at Spook. "Herbert T wants you and Dwayne wants our business."

"It don't take a motha fucka with a G.E.D. to figure out that they will try kill us all," said Spook.

Up until now Crack Pipe, Isis, and Michelle had been silent. "Baby, let us go in first. We could catch them off guard and put some hurt on them," said Isis.

Spook didn't mind any of his crew voicing their opinion as long as it had something to do with the mission. He said, "There's only one thing wrong with that Isis. We don't know where they are."

Something had been bothering Stone. He couldn't quite put his finger on it. Dwayne and Herbert T. were well informed on his comings and goings. It just didn't sit well. Something was off, but what was it?

Allen's phone rang, bringing Stone out of his train of thought. Everyone assumed it was Dwayne or Herbert T. telling him the meeting place. They knew different when Allen's eye brow shot up and a small smile creased his face.

"You sure?" Allen said into the phone. "Okay, thanks a lot. I'll get your payment to you through our usual channels." The smile remained on Allen's face as he put the phone away.

"We might have a small break. My contact saw a powder blue Hummer go into a warehouse not too far from here. It's over by the old factories where the Kalamazoo river flows. We need to move fast," said Allen.

"Not so fast mellow. This could be a trap. I'm not trying to impugn your integrity but, is this contact trustworthy? Keep in mind we trusted Dwayne. I guess what I'm saying is we need to have a plan with a plan. We need to cover all bases. We can't be too careful. We have a lot to lose, most importantly, our lives," Stone reasoned.

"So what do you have in mind?" asked Spook.

"Let's step out of the van for a second."

The three men stepped from the van and walked and talked. Crack Pipe, Michelle, and Isis watched them through the windows. It began to rain. The three men returned to the van and took their seats. The van moved down the wet and dark streets of Battle Creek as the rain poured. Finally, Allen pulled the van into one of the abandoned factory parking lots. The warehouse was about a block down the street.

Spook turned to his crew. "Okay, I'm going with Allen and Stone. I want you to stay here until we get back. Which one of you has my phone?"

"I got it Spook. I won't lose it," said Crack Pipe.

"Good, because I'll be calling you on it shortly. When I do, I want all y'all to come in blasting. Shoot anyone except me, Allen, and Stone. Do you understand?"

They all nodded their heads.

"Whoa, hold up, Spook. Delsena's in there too. She's dark skinned with long black hair, and knowing her, she's dressed real nice. Whatever you do, don't blast her. I repeat don't blast her!" said Stone. He looked at Spook for reassurance.

"Y'all heard the man. The lady is not to be harmed. She's off limits. Everyone else is fair game, understood?"

"Let's go ," said Stone.

Crack Pipe pulled out his dope.

"What the fuck are you doing? Spook told us to lay off that stuff until the mission is finished. That how we got into trouble earlier listening to yo ass. Talking about let's just take one hit. You see Spook knew we were high. Fuck that! We can wait," said Isis.

"Crack Pipe, we don't need you stuck. You could get us all killed," added Michelle.

"This lil bit ain't gone hurt anybody. What y'all gone do, tell the big bad Spook on me? Y'all need to relax. What's the sense in having this shit if you can't enjoy it. Fuck Spook, he won't be back no way. You'll see. Then all of this dope and money will be ours to do as we please," said Crack Pipe.

"What? What the fuck do you mean Crack Pipe?" asked Isis.

"Do y'all remember when Allen and Spook went in to get Stone?"

Isis and Michelle didn't say a word, they just looked at him.

"Well, Allen's phone rang. I answered it and it was Herbert T."

"When did you answer the phone?" asked Michelle.

Isis chimed in, "Yeah, we didn't see you answer no phone."

"You bitches never pay me any attention, especially when y'all getting high. Y'all be so much into each other's pussies, you wouldn't know if a meteorite hit. Anyway

Herbert T. made me an offer. I told him what happened at the house. I even left the phone on so he could hear all of us talking on the ride back. Herbert T. Promised to take care of me real swell."

Crack Pipe put fire to his pipe. He filled his lungs with smoke. He continued, "One thing I've learned from Spook is to take care of yours. Now I've got to call Herbert T. and let him know Spook, his brother, and Stone are on their way. Are you girls with me?"

"You super stupid motha fucka. Spook takes care of us and he treats us good. Damn you! What have you done? That's the man I love. The man I would die for. You son of a bitch," said Isis. She went for her gun.

Crack Pipe had learned a lot from Spook, especially how to be controlling. Fuck these hoes. Crack Pipe's gun lay between his legs. He drew down on Isis before she could pull her gun out. "Isis, you're my sister but I will kill you. Take your hand from yo purse. Now!"

Isis hesitated.

"I ain't playing girl. Take yo hand out and throw yo purse over here or I'll shoot you dead."

Isis was pissed. Spook would either get killed or kill them all when he returned. She did as Crack Pipe asked.

Crack Pipe turned to Michelle, "Now, you do the same. I won't ask you twice. Me and you have no blood ties. I'll shoot yo ass for the hell of it."

Michelle threw her purse on the van's floor at his feet. "Man you trippin. You really shouldn't be doing this man. It'll come back and bite you in the ass," said Michelle. She wanted to beat his ass. She had fire in her eyes.

"Both of you once a month bleeding, cum burping, bitches are the one's that's tripping. Y'all can roll with me while these motha fucka's kill themselves. We could have it all. Hell Isis, you know before I started using, I was the stick up kid. I took shit from motha's all the time. Y'all think I'm gone settle for the crumbs when I can have the whole cake? Shit, I want it all.

"Now y'all can roll with me or get fucked over. Cause I'm gone take this van and what we got in it and come up in this bitch. Y'all think Crack Pipe ain't nothing but a dope fiend? I just lay back waiting on a motha fucka to slip. Now what y'all gone do?"

"Yo ass talking a whole bunch of high powered shit," said Michelle. She attempted to rush him. The van made her moves awkward. She had to hunch down and try to move fast. Crack Pipe never moved from his seat. He just extended his foot sideways real fast and caught Michelle in her stomach. She folded over with his Isis behind her. Crack Pipe thumped the hammer back on his gun and aimed it at Isis. She stopped her dead in her tracks. Michelle was trying to catch her breath when Crack Pipe hit on the side of her head with the gun.

The blow sent her stumbling back to the seat from which she came. She collided with Isis along the way. Michelle held the side of her head. Isis straightened herself as best

266

she could and helped Michelle lay back in her seat. She could see the damage Crack Pipe had done to Michelle's head.

All of a sudden the sliding door opened. Strong hands lifted Crack Pipe from his seat. Crack Pipe's gun hit the pavement. He came crashing down to the wet ground next. The landing took his breath away.

The girls had been seized with panic until they realized it was Spook. They recovered their guns and got out of the van. They saw Spook standing over Crack Pipe. Stone and Allen stood to the side.

Spook looked down at Crack Pipe. He wanted to crush him with the heel of his shoe. "I heard everything," he said.

"You thought we had left, but were out here listening the whole time," said Allen.

"We didn't know which one of you was leaking information," said Spook

"So how did you know it was ..." began Crack Pipe.

Stone interrupted, "How did we know it was you? Dwayne said something that started me to thinking. How did he know Tomorrow was dead? The only people who knew that were in the van. So we set our own little trap for your ass."

When Stone finished his sentence, Crack Pipe was in a sitting position. His gun was within arms reach. Spook was surprised that Crack Pipe would draw down on him.

He was taken off guard. That gained Crack Pipe the extra seconds he needed. Crack Pipe 's hand had closed around his gun just as Spook hand reached his own gun. Crack Pipe's finger was on the trigger. A shot fired. Spook thought he was hit.

Crack Pipe's gun dropped from his hand. He put his hand over the bloody hole in his chest. Isis stood wide legged with her gun smoking in her hand.

Crack Pipe turned his head to see who shot him in his back. You shot me. Your own brother. I can't believe you shot me." He lost all consciousness as his blood mixed with the rain soaked asphalt.

Spook went to Isis' side while Stone and Allen dragged Crack Pipe's body into an abandoned building. Michelle hugged and kissed Isis on her cheek. She returned to the van to give her and Spook a moment together.

"Baby you did what you had to do," said Spook.

Isis said, "I know. I ain't trippin'. I just couldn't stand the thought of losing you."

"You gonna be okay?"

"Yeah I'll be fine. I mean we both gave him a way out, but greed motivated him to cross us all. He made his choice."

"Okay, we'll talk more later. Here come Allen and Stone. Get back in the van. You and Michelle keep yall guns handy. I might still need you. Here, hang on to my phone. If I call, just come in."

Allen, Stone, and Spook made their way to the warehouse on foot. A couple of cars went by them. One was a red Ford Mustang. Two young boys were inside the car. Rap music played ridiculously loud. The car slowed, the boys looked at the men, and then sped away.

"I'm glad to many cars don't come this way," said Allen

"I'm hoping that gunshot didn't announce our arrival," said Stone.

"I kind of doubt it concerned the police on this side of town. Let's hope it didn't put Herbert T. and Dwayne on alert," added Allen.

Spook noticed a Lexus in front of the warehouse. Two men stood beside the car. Spook stopped Stone and Allen in their path with his arm. He pointed to the car.

 The rain came down in sheets. The river could be heard running on the side of warehouse. The current was moving the water fast. It was loud as a water fall.

"I think it's safe to say the gun shot wasn't heard. It was drowned out by the water," reasoned Allen.

"How do we get passed those two goons?" asked Stone.

Spook bent down and splashed some muddy water on himself. He also untucked his shirt. "Stay here. I got this," said Spook. He went towards the Lexus with a wet crotch. He staggered to make sure he got the attention of the men.

"Wait," Allen whispered so the men in the car wouldn't hear.

Spook could have won an Oscar for his performance as a drunken bum. He really looked the part. Spook made it to the trunk of the car when the two men saw him. They reached for their guns.

CHAPTER 30

Delsena had been silent since Herbert T. threatened to cut off her clit. Herbert T. chewed on his cigar while cleaning his nails with the switch blade. He leaned against the office door. She sat with her back to the door across the desk from Dwayne. He kept eyeing her hungrily.

He said, "Things will be alright after tonight. Your boy Stone needs to be brought down. You should be in agreement with me. I mean you are a queen and what does he do? He puts you to the side for that yellow cunt Tomorrow. Now how stupid is that? Look at yo fine ass. You're irresistible. Hell, I'd run through the jungle with a pork chop suit just to smell that pussy of yours. When all of this is over with, you and I will mix our DNA. Shit, I'm getting hard just thinking about you."

Delsena hung her head and said a silent prayer.

***

Allen and Stone's first reaction was to shoot them where they stood. Of course the gun fire would alert those inside, even the sound of raging river wouldn't cover up the noise. The men relaxed their hands. Allen and Stone let Spook do his thing.

Both men were on alert by Dwayne. They couldn't take any chances. They thought it would be a good idea to address the man. Once they saw he was drunk, no guns were necessary. There was always the chance of gunshots reaching the wrong ears.

Spook was singing out of tune with a slurred voice. "Hey, Can I get a cigarette and a light from one of y'all?" Spook swayed back and forth like he couldn't maintain his balance. Spook's hand shot out and upwards with his palm open. It connected with the man's nose. It made a crunching sound as it broke. Bone fragments went into the man's brain. He died instantly.

The other man saw what happened to his boy. He reached for his gun. Spook saw the move but didn't have time to pull his gun. Then something came flying past Spook. It made a hollow thump like a watermelon when it hit the man's forehead. The man to abandoned his attempt to reach for his gun. He howled out in pain and reached to his forehead to assess the damage. This was the break Spook needed. He stepped to the man.

The man threw a weak punch at Spook who easily blocked it. Spook countered with a left and a right. The man's eyes rolled back in his head. Spook then lifted the man with both of his hands. Lightning flashed overhead. Spook looked like something evil from a horror show. Thunder clapped when Spook broke the man's back.

Allen couldn't believe how efficient Spook killed without seeming to give it a thought. Allen would forever view his older brother in a different light.

"What did you hit that man with?" asked Spook.

Stone bent down and picked up his gun from the ground. "It was my gun. I didn't have the time to think. I just did it."

272

"Good move," said Spook.

"You're welcome. We have much to do before we break our arms patting each other on the back," replied Stone.

Stone watched out as Spook and Allen sat the men in the Lexus. At a casual glance the bodies appeared to be sleeping or in a nod from drugs. The rain didn't seem to be letting up. Big drops soaked through their clothes. Stone saw a red Mustang slow down. Was it the same Mustang that passed them earlier? He made a mental note of it.

The warehouse was old. Broken windows were here and there. They entered through one of the windows on the side. Most of the warehouse was dark. That was good. They could move about under cover of darkness. Then they saw the Hummer parked by the loading area. Spook removed the plastic explosives from the pocket of his cargo pants. Stone whispered, "What the fuck you are doing man?"

Spook answered, "I feel like blowing some shit up."

"Just wait until Delsena is alright before you all suicide bomber on me."

"I'm tired of pussy footing with these motha fucka's. I want to bring some serious pain to these boys. Believe me, I won't do nothing to hurt this," said Spook pointing to himself.

"Stone's right Spook. We should wait until she's safe. Besides, you'll blow us all to hell with that shit," added Allen.

273

"I'm only gonna use a fraction of what I have. I going to put half a bar of soap size piece under the gas tank. I'll set the timer for fifteen minutes. That should distract them for a moment."

Allen knew this to be the best course of action because they didn't completely know what they were up against. All three men knew the most carefully thought out plans could go wrong. You could be 99% sure of your great plan, but it's the unknown factor that could be get you killed. Right now they could use all the help they could get.

"Do it," said Stone. He wished to get this ordeal over with.

"Listen, this is very important. Be anywhere but here when this goes off." Spook set the explosives near the Hummer's gas tank and set the timer. Each man looked at his watch.

Allen pointed to a light on the second floor. They could see Herbert T. leaning against the doorframe smoking a cigar. Dwayne had his feet on the desk. Part of a woman's head could be seen too. There wasn't a doubt in Stone's mind that It was Delsena .

There were stairs on the left and stairs on the right. Both led straight to office where the two men and Delsena were. The men made their way up the steps being ever so careful not to make any sound. They closed in on both sides.

They were close enough to hear Dwayne say, "Let's give them sucka's a call."

The thought occurred to Allen but it was too late. His phone rang loud enough to reach Dwayne and Herbert T.

CHAPTER 31

"What the Hell?" said Herbert T. He looked in the direction of the sound. He saw Allen and Stone coming up the stairs. The element of surprise was exposed. Dwayne jumped from his chair and ran to Herbert T's side. None of the men wanted to shoot for fear of hitting Delsena.

Herbert T. threw his switch blade at Stone and Allen. The hurried throw was off target. It flew over their heads. He went for his gun. Spook was at the top of the other staircase. He charged at Herbert T. Spook grabbed the hand that Herbert T. held the gun in. They wrestled over the gun. When they bumped into Dwayne it caused a domino effect. Spook and Herbert T. pushed Dwayne to the edge of the stairs. Dwayne fell on top of Stone. Stone fell on Allen. They all rolled down the stairs. Spook and Herbert T. tumbled down behind them.

Allen's head banged on the ground. He was knocked out for the count. Stone landed on top of Dwayne. Herbert T's gun discharged during the fight against gravity and the steps. Spook was shot in the shoulder.

Stone was a bit disoriented but managed to get on his knees. He pulled out the twins. He quickly placed them against Dwayne's chest.

"Do it and I'll blow this lame's head off," said Herbert T. His gun was pointed at Spook 's head.

"Do it. I'll kill Dwayne and maybe have enough time to squeeze off a shot at you," said Stone.

"Looks like we have a standoff," said Dwayne. He wasn't sure if Stone would shoot.

Stone said, "Let Delsena go."

"Let Dwayne go or I'll put one in his melon. I don't like this motha fucka no way," replied Herbert T.

Stone knew they were too close to the Hummer. It was going to explode soon.

Delsena could see and hear what was going on. Her heart leaped with joy when she seen it was Stone. She thought it was best to stay put for the moment.

"Stone, I ain't no damn fool. Who do you think you fuckin with? Let him go and drop your guns or I'll shoot this black ass motha fucka. You know that I will do it."

"Stone, we don't have time for this shit. Do as he says and make sure Allen's okay," said Spook.

Stone knew what Spook meant. He meant get Allen to a safe distance before the C4 detonated.

"Alright. I'm putting my guns down," said Stone.

Stone put both guns on the floor, held his hands, took a couple steps back, and stooped down to check on Allen. Dwayne grabbed the guns and put his gun back in the waistband of his pants. Dwayne stood up and pointed the guns at Stone. Herbert T. and Spook stood too. Allen starting to come around.

"Me and Spook are going to take a ride. You can handle things from here, can't you?" said Herbert T. He nudged Spook with his gun towards the Hummer.

"Yeah I got this. Hey Spook, just so you know, I followed you and Lisa that night. I waited until you left, went up there, and I beat her bad. I took the pussy while she was passed out. I knew you'd get the blame. I used a rubber so no DNA will be found. I knew this would mess you up with your brother and everyone else. No one likes rapist. I just wanted you to know. Enjoy what Herbert T. has in store for you," said Dwayne. He had no regrets.

Allen, Stone, Spook, and Delsena were stunned.

"Get in, you're driving us somewhere that I've designed just for you. I call it my house of pain," sneered Herbert T.

Spook didn't want to get into the Hummer. It was a death trap. He knew if he didn't, they all would be killed in a matter of minutes. He looked at Stone and said, "Take care of Allen." He got in the S.U.V. with Herbert T.

"You take care of you. I got Allen," replied Stone before they closed the doors on the Hummer.

Dwayne said, "Ain't that touching? You ain't safe your damn self. Help Allen up, you two are going up with me. I got some paperwork for you two sign saying that you're turning everything over to me. This way it's legal." He pointed one gun at Stone and the other at Allen.

Herbert T. used the remote to open the freight door so the Hummer could leave. The engine was running and Spook had it in drive with his foot on the gas pedal. He wanted to get the explosive away from his brother. Spook didn't mind dying but he would save his brother at all cost. Just when he was inching the big vehicle forward, a female stepped into the opening. It was Isis. She had her gun pointed at the windshield in her wide legged stance.

The next events happened fast. Isis took in everything she saw. She saw Stone pull Allen to his feet. She saw the man holding a gun on them. She saw the man pointing a gun at Spook's head.

Spook stole a glance at his watch. They had less than thirty seconds before the Hummer blew. Spook said softly to himself "Move Isis baby. Please move."

Isis hesitated at shooting for fear of hitting Spook. Herbert T. wanted to shoot her through the windshield, but thought of something better. Herbert T. removed the gun from Spook's head and fired a round in to Spook thigh. The muscle reflex caused Spook to extend his leg and apply pressure to the gas pedal. The tires screamed. The big monster jumped forward at a fast clip.

Spook's tried to steer. Isis never had a chance. The hummer slammed into her. The metal came into contact with flesh and bones. The impact broke most of her bones and threw her into the air. What was left of her came to rest in the angry river. Herbert T. smiled.

Allen, was awake and on his feet. He witnessed the horrific slaying of Isis with Stone and Dwayne. The powder blue Hummer went down the street towards the small bridge.

"That's what that bitch get. Who the fuck she thought she was? Both of you, up stairs," said Dwayne. Stone started up the stairs. They made it to the office door when they heard a huge explosion. Boom! They all turned to see the Hummer going up in flames. All that was left was a twisted skeleton of metal among the smoke and flames.

Dwayne saw movement from the corner of his eye. It was a white girl. She ran in during the explosion. She was making her way behind him. Dwayne didn't let on that he'd seen her. He herded them into the office then he turned quickly shot where he last saw Michelle. Dwayne pushed Allen and Stone so he could come into the office and close the door.

He knew that a white girl was out there with a gun. What Dwayne didn't know was Delsena was hiding behind the door. She held a big ash tray in her hands. She was standing in a chair. Stone and Allen saw her before Dwayne. Del brought the ashtray down hard on his forehead. Stone dived at Dwayne. He grabbed him around his waist and they hit the floor.

Both guns slid by Allen's feet. Allen grabbed both. Delsena watched the two men were locked into mortal combat. Allen couldn't shoot Dwayne without hitting Stone in the process. Also his vision was off due to his fall down the stairs. He was seeing double and had to hold on to the edge of the desk. He felt light headed and dizzy. He was suffering from a mild concussion. Delsena went to help Allen maintain his balance.

Stone and Dwayne squared off face to face. Stone head butted Dwayne, forcing him to let go of him. Then Stone followed up with a combinations of punches that backed up Dwayne against the window. Dwayne swung at Stone who ducked the punch. Stone came back with a strong upper cut. Dwayne's head snapped back. Stones kicked Dwayne in his mid section with all his might. Dwayne folded over.

Stone thought about all the death and pain that this man had brought into his life in such a short time. Dwayne reached for the gun in his pants. Stone ran forward. He kicked Dwayne in his face. The big man flew back into the window. The glass broke and pieces of glass followed him as he screamed all the way down. He hit the frigid water. Stone, Allen, and Delsena looked down at the deep, fast flowing, unforgiving water. It was impossible to swim in it. Delsena hugged Stone tight. and then they helped Allen to the door.

"Michelle, we're coming out! Can you hear me?" yelled Stone.

Michelle didn't answer.

"Michelle, we're coming down," Stone yelled again.

They helped Allen down the stairs. Stone went to where they heard the crying. Michelle was standing against the wall crying. Delsena went to comfort her.

"Thank you for helping us. " said Delsena.

"Spook and Isis got killed," said Michelle between sobs.

"Michelle, Stone and I thank you too. You know that Spook was my brother. He died saving us. I also feel a great loss. You can come with us if you'd like," said Allen.

"Yes, I guess I can do that for now," replied Michelle.

Sirens could be heard in the distance. They were getting closer.

***

Spook felt he could cry knowing Isis died at his hands or more to the point, his foot. He was with a man that he wanted to kill so badly, he could taste it. The C4 would explode any minute. He had nothing to lose. Staying in the Hummer was a sure death. Herbert T. wasn't wearing his seat belt.

Spook braced himself by gripping the steering wheel. He slammed on the brakes. The Hummer came to a sudden stop. Herbert T. slammed against the windshield and discharged his weapon. The bullet grazed Spook's forehead and shattered the window on his side. Spook opened the door and jumped. The pavement gave no pardon to his landing. It tore the skin from his arms and head as he rolled.

The Hummer coasted forward over the bridge. The vehicle detonated before Herbert T. could climb into the driver's seat to gain control of the runaway vehicle. Spook laid on the bridge. The wind was knocked out of him. He had bullet holes in his shoulder and thigh. He also had scrapes and scratches over most of his body. The rain that fell was soothing to his skin. He ignored the police sirens he heard in the distance.

***

The small group headed out of the warehouse. They saw a figure on the bridge. It was Spook. Michelle ran to him. She was so happy to see him she almost knocked him over with her hug. Delsena and Stone helped Allen along toward Spook. He was about fifty yards away.

A car skidded to a stop on the opposite side of the street from Spook. A young man stepped from the car. He had a gun. Spook had no idea who this young man was. Spook pushed Michelle away. She hit the ground hard.

"Yeah Motha fucka," the young man said as he aimed at Spook. "I'm going to kill yo bitch ass. Lisa is my mother. You raped her! You bastard."

Stone and Allen both yelled at the same time, "Jason!"

Jason didn't want to hear anything. He didn't want to talk. He was fueled by a desire for revenge. Jason fired twice. The first bullet sailed past Spook. The second found its mark. It hit Spook in the right upper side of his chest. Stone let go of Allen and ran to Spook. Allen saw the red circle get bigger on Spook's chest. Spook leaned over the railing and fell off the bridge.

Allen fell from Delsena's grip to his knees screaming, "NOOOOOOOOOOOOO!"

Michelle's face filled with anger and rage. She pulled her gun and squeezed round after round into the teenager's body. His body jerked as she emptied her gun. Jason fell face first into the street. Michelle threw her gun into the river. She looked over the bridge where Spook had fallen. He was barely hanging on to the edge. She climbed over the bridge and extended her hand to him. She used all of her strength to pull her big man.

Delsena and Allen made it to Stone. They watched Michelle and Spook. The water moved swiftly and you could see ice on the river bank. If the fall didn't kill you, the cold water would. Hypothermia had claimed many lives. Stone knew this because when he was into his addiction, one of his get high buddies died from it. He was in an abandoned house that had no heat in the dead of winter. His body temperature had dropped abnormally low and his heart stopped beating.

"Hold on Spook. I'm on the way," said Allen.

Allen tried to get to the side of the bridge to help his brother. He slipped and almost fell into the icy water. Stone grabbed Allen and pulled him back. Stone said, "Your balance is off Allen. You stay, I'll go."

Michelle stained to pull Spook. She had one of his arms. Spook managed to hold onto the bridge. He was losing blood and weakening by the minute. He didn't have enough strength left to pull himself up.

Two police cars pulled up. The officers jumped from the cars and ran to the railing with their guns drawn. The police saw the S.U.V. and Jason's bullet riddled body in the street. They decided to keep the group covered until back up arrived. These people had a lot of explaining to do.

"Spook hang in there. Michelle you done good," said Stone. He gripped Spook's forearm and began to pull him up.

Spook looked at the police and then he looked at Allen. "I love you baby brother." He let go of Stone's hand and fell into the icy water below.

Michelle did a swan dive in the water after Spook. Everyone looked on in awe as the water thrashed about violently and the current took them both downstream.

Stone, Allen, and Delsena were taken down to the police station. They were questioned by the police. Stone and Allen explained but left out certain incriminating parts. Herbert T. and Dwayne were wanted back in Detroit for a host of felonies. The prosecutor declined to prosecute since none of them had criminal records. Delsena was an outstanding pillar of the community. The following morning they all walked out the police station.

Delsena and Carol became tight friends over the next months. Everyone, including Delsena, mourned the loss of Tomorrow. Isis was recovered from the river. Allen paid for her funeral. Spook and Michelle were never found. Crack Pipe was never mentioned. The whereabouts of his body were unknown. Dwayne's body never turned up either. Rumor had it that he was living in New York.

Seven months later Stone and Delsena got married. So did Allen and Carol. It was double wedding. The biggest wedding that most had seen. Stone mother was there. She was pleased to see her son so happy. The couples sneaked out the back of the church for a stroll. They laughed and hugged each other.

Carol, Allen, and Stone rubbed Delsena's stomach. She was carrying Stone's child. She had a pregnant woman's glow. All it took was a successful operation to prove she could have children.

"Carol, my wife, you make me feel so alive," said Allen.

"I love you baby," replied Carol. She kissed Allen softly.

"Honey, you've made me the happiest woman on earth," said Delsena.

"Delsena, you are so wonderful. I've been blessed with you and out child. I give God all the praise," replied Stone. He looked into her eyes and kissed her.

"What time is it?" asked Delsena.

Stone looked at his watch, "8:31. Why?"

"Because we all just kissed our mates at the same time. We'll do it on our anniversary every year, even if we stay on different ends of the world. Friends for life."

Carol said, "That sounds like a great idea. I don't know why I didn't think of it."

Both women grabbed their husband by the face and planted a wet kiss that took their breath away. Then both women wiped their lipstick form their husband lips.

They all walked hand in hand back to the church. The reception was underway. Allen's phone rang.

"I thought I turned this thing off," said Allen. He took the phone from his pocket. "Hello."

The voice said, "Congratulations little brother"

"Spook!" Allen was overwhelmed by the surprise.

Stone, Delsena, and Carol stopped in their tracks at the sound of Spook's name.

"Yeah, it's me. I can't stay on too long for obvious reasons."

"We thought you were dead. We all thank you from the bottom of our hearts. I love you man."

"Yeah we love you Spook," Spook heard the others in the background.

"How did you survive?" asked Allen.

"Michelle saved my life. She use to be a surgical nurse before she started using and lost her job. She also worked as a lifeguard when she was a teenager. Man she swims like a fish. Any way she nursed be back to health. We're together. I just wanted to congratulate you and let you know that I'm doing fine," said Spook.

"Tell Michelle thanks. How did you know I was getting married today?"

"You're my baby brother. I be keeping tabs on yo ass. Kiss Carol and Delsena for me. Tell Stone he has my blessing. I really must go. Oh, Michelle sends her love."

"Spook just knowing that you're alive is the best wedding gift I could ever have. Will I ever see you again?"

"In due time I will be seen again. In due time. I love you baby brother." Spook hung up the phone.

Tears of joy escaped from Allen's eyes. Allen told them about Spook as they headed inside. A shot was heard and Stone fell in the grass. Crack Pipe stood there with a gun.

" Y'all thought I was dead, huh? How y'all gonna leave me for dead in a tore up ass building? Well any way I'm here to get paid from all of you motha fucka's. Y'all owe me," said Crack Pipe. He looked awful. There was a white crusty substance around his ashy lips. He looked like a bum.

His gun was trained on Allen. Delsena bent down to check on her husband.

"Leave him. I hope I killed him. He spoiled my plans. Dwayne and Herbert T. would have made me rich by now."

Allen was furious. He didn't have his gun. Why should he? It was their wedding day. "This our wedding day, if he's dead I will…."

Crack Pipe didn't let Allen finish his sentence. "Shut the fuck up. I don't give a fuck about a wedding. If I did, I wouldn't be here with a gun in my hand now would I?"

The wedding guests heard the gun shot. They filed out the church to see what was going on.

"Stay over there everyone," yelled Allen.

They all saw the man with the gun. They didn't need to be told twice. Crack Pipe waved his gun in their direction. Carol and Delsena looked at each other. Stone moaned and turned over. Crack Pipe was startled by Stone's movement. He made up his mind to just shoot them all. Giving Stone all of his attention was a fatal mistake on his part.

Carol and Delsena both reached under their wedding dresses and pulled out nickel plated .380's. They fired shot after shot in Crack Pipe. His body dropped. He lay there dead as his red blood soaked into the green grass. Stone got to his feet. He only had a flesh wound. There was a small scar across his forehead.

"You played dead?" said Allen.

"Yeah, I thought it best to play it by ear. My mind is made up to enjoy life regardless of life's hardships. I'm not letting anything ruin this day. What possessed you girls brings guns to our wedding?" asked Stone.

"Yeah, that's a damn good question," added Allen.

"It was Delsena's idea and I stand with her on it," said Carol.

"Yeah with you two as our men, we can't take chances. I've learned to always be prepared. No one, and I do mean no one will take our happiness," said Delsena. She waved her gun in the air.

The girls put the guns back under their dresses.

The wedding crowd had gathered around them. Sirens could be heard by everyone except the two couples. They were lost inside the hugs and kisses of their spouses.

www.ingramcontent.com/pod-product-compliance
Lightning Source LLC
Chambersburg PA
CBHW072114270326
41931CB00010B/1556